AINSLEY HARRIOTT'S
COMPLETE GOURMET EXPRESS

AINSLEY HARRIOTT'S
COMPLETE GOURMET EXPRESS

BBC

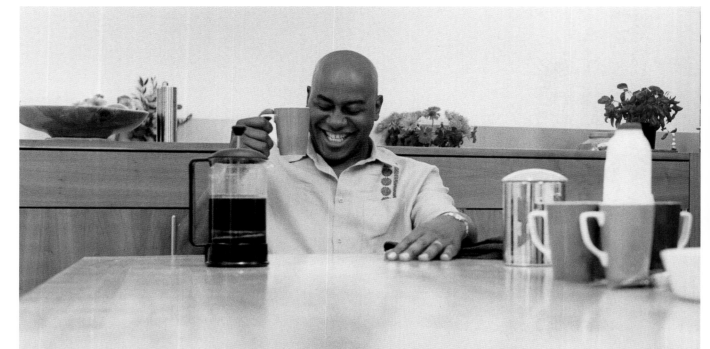

This edition is specially produced for WHSmith to accompany the television series *Gourmet Express*, first broadcast in 2000, and *Gourmet Express 2*, first broadcast in 2001.

The series were produced by BBC Birmingham.
Executive Producer: Nick Vaughan-Barratt
Executive Editor: Franny Moyle
Series Producer: Sara Kozak
Director: Stuart Bateup

Published by BBC Worldwide Ltd, 80 Wood Lane, London W12 0TT

Gourmet Express was first published in 2000
Gourmet Express 2 in 2001
This edition was first published 2003 © Ainsley Harriott 2000, 2001 and 2003.
The moral right of the author has been asserted.

ISBN 0 563 52128 7

Recipes developed and written in association with Silvana Franco
Studio photographs by Gus Filgate © BBC Worldwide Ltd 2000 and 2001.

Location photography by Craig Easton © BBC Worldwide Ltd 2000 and 2001.

Commissioning Editors: Nicky Copeland and Rachel Copus
Project Editors: Rachel Copus and Rebecca Hardie
Cover Art Director: Pene Parker
Book Art Directors: Lisa Pettibone and Sarah Ponder
Designers: John Calvert and Susannah Good
Food Stylists: Silvana Franco assisted by Sharon Hearne and Nicola Kelly
Food Stylists for location photographs: Jenny White and Clare Lewis
Props Stylist: Penny Markham
Production Controller: Kenneth McKay

Set in Eurostile and Humanist
Printed and bound in Great Britain by Butler & Tanner Ltd, Frome and London
Colour origination by Radstock Reproduction Ltd
Cover printed by Lawrence Allen Ltd

All the spoon measurements in this book are level unless otherwise stated.
A tablespoon is 15 ml; a teaspoon is 5 ml. Follow one set of measurements when preparing any of the recipes. Do not mix metric with imperial. All eggs used in the recipes are medium sized. All vegetables should be peeled unless the recipe says otherwise.

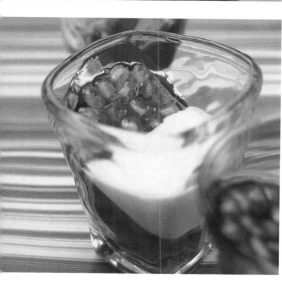

CONTENTS

INTRODUCTION

If you've had a hard day working at home, or in the office, or looking after the kids, there's always another job that awaits you – cooking an evening meal. And sometimes, let's face it, being creative is the last thing on your mind. For an instant quick fix, you could order a take-away, or bung a ready-made meal in the microwave, but these dishes are often unappetizing, quite pricey, and not always very nutritious.

Well, don't worry. Help is at hand! *Ainsley Harriott's Complete Gourmet Express* brings together for the first time my two books *Gourmet Express* and *Gourmet Express 2* in one handy volume. It's full of interesting, easy-to-make meals that have the right balance of colour, texture and flavour and taste great. So, before you pick up that phone or set the microwave timer, have a look at the wonderful recipes I've included here – they're sure to inspire you.

There are ideas to suit every occasion and everyone's tastes, including quick snacks, soups to go, starters, hearty mains, including a choice of vegetarian dishes, side orders, and of course, wicked desserts! What's more, they have all been tried and tested, tasted and tweaked to perfection. It was a real pleasure entertaining friends and family who were only too happy to give me an instant reaction to the food – y'know, 'hmmm, that's lovely', 'oooh, that's gorgeous', or 'Ains, this is well wicked!' It's always nice to be complimented on your food; it gives you a real buzz.

I've taken on board food from all over the world to produce a range of diverse, exciting, and above all, accessible recipes. Just wait till you try my *Celtic Samosas*, *Lightning Lamb Cassoulet*, *Cracked Tapas Patatas Bravas*, *Nori-rolled Sushi*, and *Mama's Greek Butter-bean Salad*. There are also a few classics from our own back garden, like *Gina's Classic Super Shepherd's Pie*.

Food has never been more exciting or inspiring than it is today, and we can now get fresh produce from all over the world in our local shops and supermarkets – hooray! In *Ainsley Harriott's Complete Gourmet Express* I've combined lots of those fresh ingredients with store-cupboard essentials, an approach that fits in with the busy modern lifestyle. Whether you're standing with a plate full of grub, fork in hand, watching the telly, lazing on the sofa with a delicious bowl of pasta and catching up on a new CD, feeding the family at the dining table, or having friends around for supper, you'll always find something sensational to titillate those taste buds.

So, remember to stock up on those store-cupboard goodies, and you'll never be short of ideas at meal times – especially with my *Complete Gourmet Express* by your side.

Now, before we even start, here's a little something to get you going and give you lots of confidence. **Spoon Crab Canapés** are the perfect way to begin a casual dinner party.

To make enough canapés for six people, all you need to do is mix together 15 g (5 oz) fresh or canned white crabmeat, with 2 chopped salad onions, ¼ teaspoon cayenne pepper and 2 tablespoons crème fraîche. Add a little salt and pepper and a squeeze of lemon juice to taste, and chill the mixture until you're ready to serve. When your guests are about to arrive, divide the crab mixture between 12 teaspoons, then top each one with a spot of chilli sauce and a chervil leaf. Arrange on a platter and serve. What could be easier than that?

Have fun…it's only food, so enjoy the experience. Happy, smelly cooking!

Love

AINSLEY HARRIOTT'S

GOURMET EXPRESS 1

CHAPTER ONE SNACK ATTACK

Sage and onion bhajis

Genuine bhajis are made with gram flour, from chick peas. I've decided to go for a bit of a cheat's version by using regular white flour and getting the yellow colour from turmeric. I've made them even more English by adding the classic onion sidekick, sage, and it really tastes fantastic – especially with a good dollop of Maddie's Mango Chutney (page 138) or Lovely Tomato Chutney (page 142).

PREPARATION: 10 minutes COOKING TIME: 5 minutes

SERVES 2

50 g (2 oz) self-raising flour

¼ teaspoon ground turmeric

½ red chilli, finely chopped

10 sage leaves, shredded

¼ teaspoon salt

1 onion, about 100 g (4 oz), sliced

vegetable oil, for frying

METHOD

1 Place the flour, turmeric, chilli, sage and salt in a bowl. Add enough water – about 5 tablespoons – to form a very thick batter. Stir in the onion.

2 Heat 5 cm (2 inches) of oil in a wok or deep frying-pan and carefully drop the mixture into it using 2 tablespoons – 1 to scoop up the batter and the other to ease it into the oil (you might have to do this in batches). Cook for 4–5 minutes, turning occasionally, until golden brown and cooked through. Drain on kitchen paper and serve warm.

Celtic samosas

Samosas are one of my all-time favourite snacks, especially straight from the pan. I vary the filling to match my vegetable rack but I've always got a few potatoes knocking around and some peas in the freezer. My son, Jimmy, calls these 'Celtic' samosas because they're green and white inside. They're fantastic with a spoonful of Maddie's Mango Chutney (page 138).

PREPARATION: 40 minutes + 30 minutes resting COOKING TIME: 10 minutes

SERVES 4

250 g (9 oz) plain flour

2 teaspoons baking powder

½ teaspoon salt

large pinch ground turmeric

40 g (1½ oz) unsalted butter, chilled and diced

FOR THE FILLING

2 tablespoons vegetable oil

1 small onion, finely chopped

2 garlic cloves, finely chopped

1 red chilli, seeded and finely chopped

350 g (12 oz) floury potatoes, cubed and boiled

75 g (3 oz) frozen peas, thawed

1 teaspoon ground cumin

salt

2 tablespoons chopped fresh coriander

vegetable oil, for deep-frying

METHOD

1 Sift the flour, baking powder, salt and turmeric into a bowl. Using your fingers, rub the butter into the flour until the mixture resembles breadcrumbs. Stir in about 150 ml (¼ pint) of water to make a soft dough. Knead well for a few minutes, then roll into 8 balls. Cover with a damp cloth and set aside for 30 minutes.

2 Heat the oil in a large frying-pan and cook the onion, garlic and chilli for 3–4 minutes until softened and golden. Add the potatoes, mashing down roughly with a fork. Add the peas, cumin and salt to taste; remove from the heat and stir in the coriander.

3 Heat about 5 cm (2 inches) of oil in a wok or deep-frying-pan. Meanwhile, roll out each piece of dough into a 10 cm (4 inch) round. Spoon an eighth of the potato mixture into the centre of each round. Moisten the edge of each round with a little water, then fold over the dough to enclose the filling, pressing the edges to seal, then gently flatten out each samosa. Fry the samosas in batches for about 2 minutes, turning until crisp and golden brown. Drain on kitchen paper and eat warm.

Hot crispy
Cajun chicken sandwich

This is one of my favourite ever late-night snacks. I vary the ingredients, depending on what's in the fridge, but all you really need is a skin-on chicken breast and a couple of slices of bread, then make up the trimmings as you go along. Other good things to put in a hot chicken sandwich include sliced gherkins, grainy mustard, sweet chilli sauce, sliced cheese or soft cheese with a shake of Tabasco.

PREPARATION: 10 minutes COOKING TIME: 15 minutes

SERVES 1

1 boneless, skin-on chicken breast

1 teaspoon Cajun seasoning, or ½ teaspoon Chinese five-spice powder and a pinch of cayenne pepper

salt and freshly ground black pepper

juice of ½ lemon (optional)

50 g (2 oz) mild blue cheese

1 tablespoon mayonnaise

4 cherry tomatoes, halved, or 1 small tomato, sliced

1 salad onion, sliced, or a few dice of raw onion

handful of salad leaves, if available

2 slices of bread

METHOD

1 Season the chicken with spice, salt and pepper. Cook skin-side down in a non-stick frying-pan for 5 minutes so the skin is nicely brown and crispy, then turn and cook for about another 4 minutes until cooked through but still moist and juicy. Now squeeze over a little lemon juice – a shake or two will do.

2 While the chicken is cooking mash together the blue cheese and mayonnaise.

3 Layer the salad ingredients on top of one of the slices of bread and top with the moist chicken followed by the blue cheese mayo. Sandwich together with the remaining bread and eat warm.

TRY THIS: Use different types of bread – French bread or pitta is equally delicious.

Hot crispy Cajun chicken sandwich

NYC foolproof falafel
with yoghurt drizzle

Real falafel have to be made with dried chick peas because the texture given by canned ones is just too soft. I've cooked many versions in the past and this is an authentic recipe – just pop a few falafel into a warmed pitta, top with a drizzle of yoghurt dressing and a pickled chilli and you'll get a snack that tastes every bit as good as one you'd buy on a New York street corner.

PREPARATION: 15 minutes + overnight soaking   COOKING TIME: 15 minutes

SERVES 4–6 (makes 16 falafel)

225 g (8 oz) dried chick peas, soaked overnight in water

1 teaspoon salt

1 teaspoon baking powder

1 teaspoon cumin seeds

1 teaspoon ground coriander

½ teaspoon cayenne pepper

1 garlic clove, crushed

2 tablespoons chopped fresh parsley

juice of ½ lemon

vegetable oil for frying

pitta bread and natural yoghurt, to serve

METHOD

1 Drain the chick peas and place in a food processor with the salt, baking powder, cumin, coriander, cayenne, garlic, parsley and lemon juice. Whizz until very finely chopped but not puréed. (If you have time, set the mixture aside for a couple of hours so that the flavours can mingle, but it's not imperative.)

2 Heat 5 cm (2 inches) of oil in a deep frying-pan or wok.

3 Using wet hands, shape the mixture into 16 balls, then flatten slightly into patties. Deep-fry in batches for about 4 minutes, turning occasionally until browned. Remove with a slotted spoon and drain on kitchen paper.

4 Serve 3 or 4 falafel inside a warm pitta bread pocket, with a drizzle of yoghurt over.

Olé nachos Mexicanos

This incredibly quick snack is easy to make at any time, but especially when my mates pop round to watch the footie: 'Did you see him save that?' Olé!

PREPARATION: 5 minutes COOKING TIME: 5 minutes

SERVES 2

150 g bag tortilla chips

200 g can chopped tomatoes

salt and freshly ground black pepper

4 salad onions, thinly sliced

2 mild red chillies, thinly sliced

50 g (2 oz) Gruyère or Cheddar, grated

150 g carton soured cream

METHOD

1 Pre-heat the grill to medium. Tip the tortilla chips into a large heatproof dish. Spoon over the chopped tomatoes and season lightly. Scatter over the salad onions, chillies and finally the cheese.

2 Place under the grill for 5 minutes until the cheese starts to melt and bubble. Serve warm, with the soured cream added to each mouthwatering mouthful.

TRY THIS: Take a look at the wide selection of tortilla chips now available in your local supermarket. Choosing a variety such as the 'fiery hot' or 'cooling soured cream' can really add an extra dimension to your nachos. And a sprinkling of pickled jalapeño chillies, if you can find them, add an authentic spicy bite to this great quick snack.

Tempura prawn
and vegetable treat

Tempura is a Japanese dish of battered, deep-fried slices of vegetable and prawns. There are lots of different ways of making tempura batter. I've simplified the process by dusting the vegetables in cornflour before dipping them in frothy egg white – it gives a crisp, golden result.

PREPARATION: 20 minutes COOKING TIME: 15 minutes

SERVES 4

FOR THE DIPPING SAUCE

100 ml (3½ fl oz) vegetable stock

4 tablespoons soy sauce

1 tablespoon sweet chilli sauce

2 tablespoons dry sherry

2.5 cm (1 inch) root ginger, finely grated

sprigs of coriander, to garnish

FOR THE TEMPURA

vegetable oil, for deep-frying

4 tablespoons cornflour

½ teaspoon salt

3 large egg whites

500 g (1 lb 2 oz) mixed vegetables, e.g. whole baby spinach leaves, halved mushrooms, sliced sweet potato, courgette, aubergine, red pepper

12 large, raw peeled prawns, tail section left intact

METHOD

1 To make the dipping sauce place the stock, soy sauce, chilli sauce, sherry and ginger in a large pan and bring to the boil. Simmer for 5 minutes.

2 Meanwhile, heat 4 cm (1½ inches) of oil in a wok. Mix together the cornflour and salt. Whisk together the egg whites and 4 tablespoons of very cold water until light and frothy. Dust the vegetable pieces and prawns with the cornflour, then dip in the frothy egg; deep-fry in batches for 3–4 minutes until golden. Drain on kitchen paper.

3 Pour the sauce into small bowls. Pile the vegetables on to serving plates and serve immediately with the dipping sauce.

Tempura prawn and vegetable treat

Hot-smoked salmon pâté
with toasted bagels

This is a twist on the classic New York smoked salmon and cream cheese bagel. Hot-smoked salmon is available from supermarkets and delicatessens and by mail order from various fish-smokeries.

PREPARATION: 15 minutes COOKING TIME: 5 minutes

SERVES 4

1 tablespoon olive oil

4 salad onions, thinly sliced

500 g (1 lb 2 oz) hot-smoked salmon, skinned and boned

250 g carton soft cheese

1 teaspoon creamed horseradish

dash of Tabasco

freshly ground black pepper

4 bagels

knob of butter

METHOD

1 Heat the oil in a pan and sauté the salad onions for 1 minute. Flake in the fish, then beat well, cooking for a further minute or two. Remove from the heat – if the mixture gets too hot, allow to cool slightly.

2 Add the soft cheese, horseradish, Tabasco and black pepper, and mix together until well combined.

3 Split open the bagels and lightly toast. Butter generously and serve with the hot-smoked salmon pâté and, if you like, a sprinkling of thinly sliced spring onion.

CHEF'S TIP: The hot-smoked salmon has a naturally salty flavour, so don't add extra.

Hot-smoked salmon pâté with toasted bagels

Webby cheese
and Parma flatbread

This is a wonderful casual snack that's quick and always impressive, especially with a bowl of chillied black olives. I love to use Italian Fontina cheese for this as it goes all gooey, webby and stretchy as it melts. Other good cheeses to use are mozzarella, Gruyère or even good old Cheddar.

PREPARATION: 5 minutes COOKING TIME: 5 minutes

SERVES 1

1 teaspoon Dijon mustard

2 x 20 cm (8 inch) flour tortillas

75 g (3 oz) Fontina, finely grated

2 slices Parma ham

freshly ground black pepper

1 teaspoon vegetable oil

METHOD

1 Smear the mustard on to one of the tortillas and scatter over the grated cheese, ham and plenty of black pepper. Place the second tortilla on top and press together firmly.

2 Brush a large non-stick frying-pan with the oil. Cook the sandwich for a minute or so on each side until crisp and well browned and molten inside. Cut into wedges or squares and eat warm.

TRY THIS: If you fancy pushing the boat out, layer fresh basil or rocket in with the cheese and ham.

Kofta rolls with chilli-yoghurt

These tasty little koftas are so much better than a lot of the kebabs you can buy from fast food restaurants – and, what's more, they're much better for you too. The chilli-yoghurt has a wonderful fresh flavour and really sets the whole thing off with a bang.

PREPARATION: 15 minutes COOKING TIME: 15 minutes

SERVES 4

450 g (1 lb) minced lamb

1 small onion, finely chopped

1 tablespoon chopped fresh mint

1 tablespoon chopped fresh parsley

2 teaspoons chopped fresh rosemary

½ teaspoon each mixed spice, ground coriander and ground cumin

salt and freshly ground black pepper

4 flour tortillas

1 red onion, thinly sliced into rings

FOR THE CHILLI-YOGHURT

300 g (11 oz) Greek yoghurt

3 red chillies, seeded and finely chopped

2 tablespoons chopped fresh coriander

2 garlic cloves, crushed

juice of 1 lime

pinch of caster sugar

salt and freshly ground black pepper

METHOD

1 Pre-heat the grill to high. Mix together the lamb, onion, herbs and spices and season with salt and pepper. Divide the mixture into four and, using your fingers, squeeze it around skewers to form long sausage shapes.

2 Grill the kofta kebabs for 10–12 minutes, turning occasionally, until well browned but still a little pink in the centre.

3 Make the dip: combine the yoghurt, chillies, coriander, garlic, lime juice and sugar, and season to taste.

4 Briefly warm the tortillas for a few seconds on each side in a dry, non-stick frying-pan, or for 10 seconds in a microwave, to make them soft and pliable. Place a kebab in the centre of each tortilla, pulling it off the skewer. Scatter over the onion rings, drizzle over the chilli-yoghurt and serve.

Nori-rolled sushi
with soy dipping sauce

Sushi is high fashion at the moment – not only is it very healthy, but it tastes great too. I get asked loads of questions about it, so I've included this classic recipe that is delicious and not too challenging. You really need a proper sushi-rolling mat to make this kind of sushi, but they can be bought cheaply from oriental stores.

PREPARATION: 30 minutes COOKING TIME: 15 minutes + cooling

SERVES 4

200 g (7 oz) Japanese rice

4 tablespoons white vinegar, such as rice vinegar or white wine vinegar

1 tablespoon caster sugar

1 teaspoon salt

½ cucumber, seeded

1 avocado

175 g (6 oz) fresh tuna or salmon

4 sheets nori seaweed

1 teaspoon wasabi paste (Japanese horseradish)

pickled ginger, to serve

Soy Dipping Sauces (page 146), to serve

METHOD

1 Begin by cooking the rice. Wash it well in warm water, then place in a pan. Cover with water so that it comes 2 cm (¾ inch) above the rice. Cover and cook gently for 12 minutes, or until the rice is tender and the water has been absorbed.

2 Meanwhile, mix together the vinegar, sugar and salt and set aside to dissolve. As soon as the rice is cooked, stir the vinegar mixture into it and leave to cool completely.

3 Cut the cucumber, avocado and fish into batons.

4 Halve the nori sheets and place one half horizontally on the rolling mat. Spread 2–3 tablespoons of the rice mixture on the seaweed, leaving a 1 cm (½ inch) margin on the edge furthest from you.

5 Spread a tiny amount of the wasabi across the centre of the rice, then place a row of cucumber and avocado or fish across the centre. Roll up so the join is on the bottom of the roll. Continue to make rolls, alternating the ingredients so that some contain just fish and others contain cucumber and avocado.

6 Trim the ends of the rolls with a sharp knife, then cut each into six pieces. Transfer to serving dishes and place a pile of pickled ginger with each. Serve with one of my Soy Dipping Sauces (page 146) – simply delicious and heavenly healthy.

Nori-rolled sushi with soy dipping sauce

Wrap and roll hot dogs
with mustard onion relish

Serving good old hot dogs in a tortilla wrap brings them right back up to date, but you can always slot them into soft finger rolls if you prefer. So come on, wrap or roll, the choice is yours.

PREPARATION: 10 minutes COOKING TIME: 20 minutes

SERVES 4

4 jumbo pork sausages

2 tablespoons olive oil

1 large red onion, thinly sliced

1 garlic clove, finely chopped

1 teaspoon yellow mustard seeds

salt and freshly ground black pepper

4 flour tortillas

Maddie's Mango Chutney (page 138), to serve

METHOD

1 Pre-heat the oven to 200°C/400°F/Gas 6. Place the sausages on a baking sheet and roast for about 20 minutes until cooked through and rich golden brown.

2 Meanwhile, heat the olive oil in a small frying-pan and cook the onion and garlic over a low heat for 10 minutes or so until soft and golden. Add the mustard seeds and cook for another couple of minutes, then season to taste with salt and pepper.

3 Place the tortilla wraps in the warm oven for a couple of minutes just to soften them up and make them easier to roll. Place a sausage in the centre of each wrap and top with a spoonful of the chutney and the mustard onion relish. Roll up and serve warm.

Late-night egg and
sausage-sizzle sarnie

When you're feeling hungry – day or night – the thought of a hot, juicy, eggy sandwich is enough to make the hair on the back of your neck stand up – what hair, Ainsley?

PREPARATION: 5 minutes COOKING TIME: 15 minutes

SERVES 1

2 teaspoons olive oil

1 pork sausage, cut into 1 cm (½ inch) pieces

2 salad onions, thinly sliced

2 eggs

2 tablespoons milk

salt and freshly ground black pepper

2 slices white bread

small knob of butter at room temperature

1 tablespoon Lovely Tomato Chutney (page 142) or brown sauce

METHOD

1 Heat the oil in a 20 cm (8 inch) frying-pan and cook the sausage for 5 minutes until golden. Add the salad onions and cook for a further minute or two.

2 Beat together the eggs, milk and some seasoning and pour over the sausage. Cook for a couple of minutes on each side until set and golden.

3 Butter the slices of bread and slide the omelette on to the unbuttered side of one of the pieces of bread. Top with the remaining slice of bread, butter-side up.

4 Cook the sandwich in the pan for 2–3 minutes on each side until crisp and golden brown. Cut in half and eat warm with the chutney or sauce.

Harissa-rubbed lamb
in charred pitta

I use lamb fillet for this dish because it's really tender, although you could use neck fillet, which is cheaper, but a little fatty (not me, the lamb). Harissa works fantastically well with lamb, though if that's not available, you could use another chilli paste. I find hummus a really good accompaniment to the lamb: you can buy it ready-made from supermarkets, or why not make your own? See my recipe for Coriander Hummus on page 37.

PREPARATION: 15 minutes COOKING TIME: 15 minutes

SERVES 4

1 tablespoon harissa or other chilli paste or sauce

juice of 1 lemon

2 tablespoons chopped fresh mint

½ teaspoon sea salt

350 g (12 oz) lamb fillets

4 pitta breads

50 g (2 oz) fresh rocket

170 g carton fresh hummus or 1 quantity of Coriander Hummus (page 37)

lemon wedges, to garnish

METHOD

1 Mix together the harissa, lemon juice, chopped mint and sea salt. Add the lamb fillets, turning to coat in the mixture, and set aside to marinate for 10 minutes or so.

2 Heat a chargrill pan for 2–3 minutes until hot. Add the lamb fillets and cook for 8–12 minutes until well browned but still a little pink in the centre; remove from the heat and allow to rest for 5 minutes to tenderize the meat. Warm the pitta in the same pan.

3 Cut the pittas in half and fill each pocket with the rocket leaves.

4 Diagonally slice the lamb into 1 cm (½ inch) thick slices and pack into the pitta. Top with a dollop of hummus and serve warm with lemon wedges for squeezing over.

Harissa-rubbed lamb in charred pitta

Coconut chicken satay pockets

Chicken fillets (the little pieces underneath regular breasts) are great for this dish because they're exactly the right size. I buy them from my local butcher, but larger supermarkets sell them in packets. If you can only get regular chicken breasts, cut them into 2 cm (¾ inch) wide strips, then bat them out with a rolling pin to flatten them slightly. The result is delicious and exquisite.

PREPARATION: 15 minutes COOKING TIME: 10 minutes

SERVES 4

200 g carton coconut cream

4 tablespoons crunchy peanut butter

2 tablespoons light soy sauce

1 tablespoon runny honey

few drops Tabasco sauce

25 g (1 oz) dry roast peanuts, roughly chopped

salt and freshly ground black pepper

250 g (9 oz) chicken fillets

4 mini naan breads, to serve

1 fresh lime, cut into wedges

METHOD

1 Pre-heat the grill to high. Soak 4 bamboo skewers in hot water.

2 Place the coconut cream and peanut butter in a bowl and beat together until well blended. Stir in the light soy sauce, honey, Tabasco and peanuts, and season to taste. If the sauce is too thick, add a little water.

3 Pour the sauce into a shallow dish and add the chicken fillets, turning to coat them in the sauce. Thread on to the skewers and cook under the grill for 4 minutes on each side until cooked through and well browned.

4 Warm the naan breads under the grill, then split in half. Remove the chicken fillets from the skewers and push them into the naan breads. Squeeze over a little lime juice and enjoy

TRY THIS: If you want to serve the filled pockets with the remaining sauce, make sure you heat it thoroughly with a little water so you can drizzle it over the chicken.

Melting mushroom
Swiss burgers

For a truly sensational burger, jazz it up with a mouthwatering topping, such as the garlic mushrooms with melted Swiss cheese described here.

PREPARATION: 15 minutes COOKING TIME: 10 minutes

SERVES 4

500 g (1 lb 2 oz) lean beef mince

4 tablespoons chopped fresh parsley

1 egg yolk

salt and freshly ground black pepper

1 tablespoon sunflower oil

4 slices Gruyère, Emmenthal or other melty Swiss cheese

4 seeded burger buns and shredded lettuce, to serve

FOR THE GARLIC MUSHROOMS

2 tablespoons olive oil

2 garlic cloves, crushed

250 g (9 oz) chestnut mushrooms, sliced

½ teaspoon cayenne pepper

METHOD

1 Mix together the mince, parsley, egg yolk and plenty of salt and pepper. Shape the mixture into 4 even-sized burgers.

2 Brush the burgers with the sunflower oil and cook on a hot griddle or in a frying-pan for 3 minutes without turning.

3 Meanwhile, heat the olive oil in a separate frying-pan and cook the garlic for 30 seconds. Add the mushrooms, cayenne and a little salt and cook for 2–3 minutes until softened and well browned.

4 Turn the burgers and lay a slice of Swiss cheese on top of each. Cook for a few more minutes until the burger is well browned but still a little pink in the centre and the cheese is beginning to soften and melt.

5 Scatter shredded lettuce over the base of each burger bun and top each with a melted Swiss cheese burger. Spoon over the garlic mushrooms, place the lid on top and serve immediately.

TRY THIS: I make a classic burger like this with pure beef, but mixing your minces can give you a really good result. Lamb is quite fatty but adds good flavour, so try half-and-half lamb and beef. Chicken and pork together and pork with sausage meat also combine to make great burgers, patties and meatballs as well as fillings for pasta dishes such as ravioli or cannelloni. Also, you could try replacing the burger buns with English muffins for a change.

Parisian
mustard sausage rolls

Fresh croissant dough is available in the chill cabinet of larger supermarkets. It's great rolled and cooked as on the packet instructions, but even better if filled with juicy sausages.

PREPARATION: 10 minutes COOKING TIME: 20 minutes

MAKES 6

1 tablespoon vegetable oil

6 pork sausages

1 x 240 g tube of chilled croissant dough

1 tablespoon Dijon mustard

1 egg yolk

pinch of salt

FOR THE DIP

4 tablespoons tomato ketchup

2 teaspoons horseradish sauce

METHOD

1 Heat the oil in a large frying-pan and cook the sausages until nicely browned; allow to cool.

2 Pre-heat the oven to 200°C/400°F/Gas 6. Open out the dough, then break along the markings to give six triangles. Smear a little mustard into the centre of each triangle, then place a sausage at the short, straight end and roll up towards the point.

3 Arrange the sausage rolls on a baking sheet. Beat together the egg yolk and salt and brush over the dough. Bake for 10–12 minutes until puffed and golden brown.

4 Meanwhile, mix together the ketchup and horseradish. Serve the sausage rolls warm with the dip.

Parisian mustard sausage rolls

Finger-lickin' chicken

Well, this is my simple but very tasty version of that famous take-away chicken dish. I actually find it a lot easier to use the oven, as you cook the whole lot in one go rather than frying it in batches, and once it's in the oven you can leave it alone – until it arrives at the table, that is.

PREPARATION: 10 minutes COOKING TIME: 40 minutes

SERVES 4

1 medium chicken cut into 8 pieces, or 8 chicken drumsticks and thighs

1 tablespoon vegetable oil

5 tablespoons plain flour

1 tablespoon Cajun seasoning

1 teaspoon cayenne pepper

½ teaspoon salt

METHOD

1 Pre-heat the oven to 220°C/425°F/Gas 7. Rub the chicken skin with the oil. Place the flour, Cajun seasoning, cayenne pepper and salt in a large bowl and mix well together.

2 Toss the chicken pieces in the flour until lightly coated. Place the chicken on a wire rack and sit the rack on a baking sheet. Cook the chicken for 35–45 minutes until cooked through with a good crispy skin; serve hot and eat with your fingers.

No-cook oh so spring rolls

I buy rice paper discs from my local oriental grocers. They're really cheap and the best thing about them is that you just need to soak them in hot water before using, although they need to be handled carefully to avoid splits. Make sure you buy the savoury variety rather than those used for biscuits and sweets. These rolls are oh so scrummy.

PREPARATION: 20 minutes

SERVES 4

7.5 x 15 cm (3 x 6 inch) rice paper wrappers

1 carrot, cut into matchsticks

10 cm (4 inch) piece cucumber cut into matchsticks

4 salad onions, shredded

1 teaspoon toasted sesame seeds

2 tablespoons hoisin sauce

350 g (12 oz) cooked chicken, shredded

METHOD

1 Place the rice paper wrappers in a heatproof bowl and cover with hot water; leave to soak for 5 minutes until soft and pliable.

2 In a separate bowl, toss together the carrot, cucumber, salad onions and sesame seeds.

3 Drain the rice papers on a clean tea towel and spread 1 teaspoon of hoisin sauce across the centre of each. Pile the vegetables and then the chicken on top.

4 Fold two sides in, then roll up to make a neat cylindrical shape. Serve within an hour or two.

CHEF'S TIP: The spring rolls are not at their best if made up too far ahead of time. Instead, prepare the vegetables and the chicken, cover separately and chill until ready to use.

Spiced, speckled
tuna mayonnaise on rye

There are lots of different rye breads available. Pumpernickel can be quite strong and crumbly in the mouth, so I prefer to use a malted rye or a sourdough bread for this special sandwich. You can also serve these as open sandwiches – just garnish with a sprig of coriander and serve with a few nice, ripe cherry tomatoes and olives.

PREPARATION: 10 minutes

SERVES 1

1 small can of tuna in brine, drained

1 shallot, very finely chopped

1 garlic clove, crushed

3 tablespoons mayonnaise

pinch of cayenne pepper

2 tablespoons chopped fresh coriander

salt and freshly ground black pepper

small knob of butter, at room temperature

2 slices light rye bread

50 g (2 oz) bag handcooked salted crisps

METHOD

1 Mix together the tuna, shallot, garlic, mayonnaise, cayenne and coriander and season to taste.

2 Butter the bread, then spread over the tuna mixture. Smash the crisps into small pieces and scatter over the tuna. Grind over a little black pepper, top with the remaining slice of bread. Cut in half and eat immediately.

Coriander hummus
with crispy garlic pitta

Hummus is wonderful spread on crackers or chunks of warm bread, or scooped up with toasted crispy garlic pitta bread.

PREPARATION: 10 minutes COOKING TIME: 5 minutes

SERVES 6

2 garlic cloves, roughly chopped

2 mild red chillies, seeded and roughly chopped

large bunch fresh coriander, roughly chopped

2 x 420 g cans chick peas, drained

juice of 1 lime

4 tablespoons olive oil

salt and freshly ground black pepper

FOR THE CRISPY GARLIC PITTA

3 tablespoons olive oil

2 garlic cloves, crushed

2 tablespoons chopped fresh parsley

4 white pitta breads

METHOD

1 Place the garlic, chillies and coriander in a food processor and whizz until finely chopped. Add the chick peas and whizz until well blended.

2 With the motor running, squeeze in the lime juice and drizzle in the olive oil to make a fairly coarse paste. Season well to taste and spoon into a serving bowl.

3 Meanwhile, mix together the olive oil, garlic and parsley and season. Heat one side of the pitta breads under a hot grill for about 1 minute until well browned.

4 Turn over the bread, then use a knife to slash the softer surface 4–5 times without cutting through the bread. Brush with the herb and oil mixture and return to the grill until bubbling and toasted (about 1 minute).

5 When cool, break into pieces and serve with the yummy hummus.

CHEF'S TIP: This is one of my favourite picnic recipes. Spoon the hummus into a lock-tight food bag and pack the pitta into an airtight box until you're ready to eat them. Don't forget to pack that crisp, chilled white wine.

Prawn
and chilli ginger cakes

These soft, fluffy fritters are delicious, especially when drizzled with my Sweet Chilli Sauce (page 147) or a squeeze of fresh lime juice.

PREPARATION: 15 minutes COOKING TIME: 10 minutes

SERVES 4 (makes 12)

2 thick slices white bread, crusts removed, about 100 g (4 oz)

250 g (9 oz) peeled raw prawns

1 green chilli, finely chopped

2.5 cm (1 inch) piece fresh root ginger, finely chopped

4 garlic cloves, finely chopped

1 tablespoon chopped fresh coriander

1 teaspoon salt

1 egg

vegetable oil for shallow-frying

baby lettuce leaves, to serve

METHOD

1 Place the bread in a bowl, cover with water, soak for about 10 seconds, then squeeze out the excess water. Place the drained bread in a food processor with the prawns, chilli, ginger, garlic, coriander, salt and egg. Pulse until well blended.

2 Heat the oil and shallow-fry spoonfuls of the mixture for 2–3 minutes on each side until puffed and golden brown. Drain on kitchen paper and serve warm on a bed of baby lettuce leaves.

Prawn and chilli ginger cakes *with* Sweet chilli sauce

Dimitri's festive feta triangles

This recipe brings back some wonderful memories of Greek holidays in Salonika – sunshine, sea and my mate Dimitri. The quantities given here will make lots of parcels, so they're perfect for serving as a starter when friends come over, or just for family nibbles. They're also great for picnics, and they freeze beautifully, too (see TRY THIS below).

PREPARATION: 30 minutes COOKING TIME: 10 minutes

MAKES 16

250 g (9 oz) feta cheese, crumbled

6 sun-dried tomatoes in oil, drained and chopped

150 g (5 oz) pitted black olives (preferably Kalamata), chopped

4 tablespoons chopped fresh parsley

2 tablespoons chopped fresh sage

½ teaspoon coarsely ground black pepper

1 tablespoon olive oil

8 sheets filo pastry, roughly 18 x 30 cm (7 x 12 inches)

50 g (2 oz) butter, melted

METHOD

1 Pre-heat the oven to 220°C/425°F/Gas 7. Mix together the feta, sun-dried tomatoes, olives, parsley, sage, pepper and olive oil.

2 Cut each sheet of pastry in half lengthways to make long strips, roughly 9 cm (3½ inches) wide. Place a spoonful of the mixture at one end of each strip and fold the corner over diagonally. Fold over again to enclose the filling and continue down the strip to make a neat, triangular parcel.

3 Transfer to a baking sheet, brush with melted butter and bake at the top of the oven for 8–10 minutes until golden brown. Serve warm.

TRY THIS: Arrange the cooked, cooled triangles on a tray and open-freeze for a couple of hours. Wrap loosely in freezer wrap and pack into a rigid plastic box or freezer bag and return to the freezer for up to one month. Defrost thoroughly before cooking.

For a nutty alternative, sprinkle a few sesame seeds on top of the triangles before baking.

Char-grilled vegetables and hummus ciabatta

Grilling vegetables releases natural sugars, which gives them a lovely charred flavour. Slap them between two pieces of sun-dried tomato ciabatta bread, add a spreading of hummus and a sprinkling of rocket or basil and you really have a very exciting eating experience.

PREPARATION: 10 minutes COOKING TIME: 15 minutes

SERVES 2

1 courgette, sliced lengthways

1 red pepper, quartered lengthways and seeded

1 tablespoon olive oil

salt and freshly ground black pepper

1 ciabatta loaf

1 sun-dried tomato in oil, finely chopped

2 handfuls rocket or a few fresh basil leaves

4 tablespoons hummus

METHOD

1 Brush the courgette and pepper pieces with oil, season and cook in a hot griddle pan or large frying-pan for 5–6 minutes on each side until softened, browned and a little charred.

2 Cut the ciabatta into 2 equal pieces, then split each half open.

3 Sprinkle the base of each half with the sun-dried tomato and scatter over the rocket or basil.

4 Arrange the char-grilled vegetables on top, then spoon over the hummus. Place the lid of the bread on top to form a sandwich, whack it in half and serve immediately.

TRY THIS: Why not try grilling other vegetables, such as aubergine, leeks, asparagus or strips of carrot?

Tomato and
feta bruschetta

Serve this snack and take a quick trip round the Med – 'bruschetta' is the Italian word for toasted bread, while rubbing the garlic over the top is very Spanish, and I've added feta and tomato for a Greek touch.

PREPARATION: 15 minutes + resting time COOKING TIME: 5 minutes

SERVES 4

250 g (9 oz) pomodorino or cherry tomatoes

200 g (7oz) feta cheese

small handful fresh mint leaves

small handful fresh basil

2–3 tablespoons olive oil

sea salt and freshly ground black pepper

1 ciabatta loaf

1 large garlic clove, unpeeled

METHOD

1 Place the tomatoes in a sturdy bowl, then use the end of a rolling pin to bash them and roughly flatten them open.

2 Crumble or roughly dice the feta into the bowl. Roughly tear in the herbs, then add 2 tablespoons of olive oil and plenty of seasoning. Set aside for at least a couple of hours.

3 Split the ciabatta in half lengthways, then cut each half widthways into 4 roughly equal-sized pieces. Drizzle the cut sides with a little olive oil and heat in a hot griddle pan or under a preheated grill until golden brown.

4 Cut the garlic clove in half and rub the cut sides over the surface of the toasted bread; sprinkle lightly with salt. Pile the tomato mixture on top and serve – a little extra coarsely ground black pepper gives the bruschetta the perfect finish.

Crispy crunchy
sweetcorn fritters

Memories of my childhood come flooding back when I think of these delightful fritters. My late mother, Peppy, would always make these for a weekend treat, accompanied with black grilled tomatoes and honey bacon. Mmmm...

PREPARATION: 5 minutes COOKING TIME: 10 minutes

SERVES 4

420 g can creamed sweetcorn

2 salad onions, finely chopped

2 tablespoons chopped fresh parsley

4–5 heaped tablespoons cornflour

salt and freshly ground black pepper

vegetable oil, for frying

soured cream, to serve

METHOD

1 Mix together the corn, salad onions, parsley, cornflour and plenty of seasoning.

2 Heat a little oil in a large frying-pan and cook large spoonfuls of the mixture for 2–3 minutes on each side until crisp and golden. Drain on kitchen paper and serve with a dollop of soured cream and a little freshly ground black pepper.

TRY THIS: Why not grill some streaky bacon until crisp and scatter on top of the soured cream?

Roasted tomato
and crème fraîche soup

Roasting the tomatoes really intensifies the flavour – and it's still a very easy soup to make. I love to serve this with Mozzamary Garlic Bread (page 122).

PREPARATION: 30 minutes COOKING TIME: 45 minutes

SERVES 4

8 ripe tomatoes, halved

1 red onion, cut into quarters

1 head of garlic, halved horizontally

2 sprigs thyme

2 tablespoons olive oil

sea salt and freshly ground black pepper

1 litre (1¾ pints) hot vegetable stock

100 g (4 oz) crème fraîche

3 tablespoons chopped fresh parsley

warm bread, to serve

METHOD

1 Pre-heat the oven to 200°C/400°F/Gas 6. Place the tomatoes, red onion, garlic and thyme in a roasting tin and drizzle over the olive oil. Season generously and roast for 30 minutes until softened and a little charred.

2 Remove the onions and garlic from the roasting tin and set aside. Pour half the stock over the tomatoes and return to the oven for 10 minutes.

3 Meanwhile, slip the onions and garlic out of their papery skins and whizz in a food processor to form a paste.

4 Remove the roasting tin from the oven, discard the thyme, then add the stock and tomatoes to the food processor, scraping up any residue with a wooden spoon.

5 Strain the mixture into a clean pan and add the remaining stock and the crème fraîche. Heat gently and season to taste. Stir in the parsley, ladle into bowls and serve with warm crusty bread.

Roasted tomato and crème fraîche soup *with* Mozzamary garlic bread

Butternut squash spiced soup

If you've not tried squash, this is a great way to enjoy it. Squash cooks down to a smooth purée, which makes for a lovely rich soup. I like to make this with butternut squash, which has great flavour, but you can use other squashes, or another delicious substitute is pumpkin.

PREPARATION: 10 minutes COOKING TIME: 40 minutes

SERVES 4

1 tablespoon olive oil

1 onion, finely chopped

1 kg (2 lb) diced squash or pumpkin

1 teaspoon cumin seeds

3 tablespoons curry paste

1 litre (1¾ pints) hot vegetable stock

275 ml carton double cream

3 tablespoons chopped fresh coriander

juice of ½ lemon

salt and freshly ground black pepper

warm naan bread, to serve

extra cream for swirling (optional but nice)

METHOD

1 Heat the oil in a large pan and cook the onion and squash or pumpkin over a gentle heat for 5–8 minutes until beginning to turn golden. Add the cumin seeds and cook for a further minute.

2 Stir in the curry paste, pour over the hot stock, cover and simmer for 30 minutes until tender.

3 Liquidize with a hand-held blender or push the mixture through a sieve. Return to the pan, stir in the cream and heat through gently. Stir in the coriander and squeeze in the lemon juice. Season with salt and pepper to taste. Ladle into bowls and serve with warm naan bread.

Easy lentil supper soup

This delicious and substantial vegetarian soup is so easy and economical to make, and it's even better on day two. My late mother used to cook it slowly with a ham hock, so for you ham lovers, simply shred up some smoked ham or pancetta and add 5 minutes before serving.

PREPARATION: 10 minutes COOKING TIME: 35 minutes

SERVES 4

1 tablespoon olive oil

1 onion, finely chopped

2 carrots, finely diced

2 garlic cloves, finely chopped

1 red chilli, seeded and finely diced

1 teaspoon yellow mustard seeds

3 tomatoes, roughly diced

100 g (4 oz) red lentils

1.2 litres (2 pints) vegetable stock

juice of ½ lemon

salt and freshly ground black pepper

METHOD

1 Heat the oil in a large pan and cook the onion and carrots for about 3–4 minutes until beginning to soften. Add the garlic, chilli and mustard seeds and cook for a further couple of minutes.

2 Stir in the tomatoes, lentils and stock and bring to the boil. Reduce the heat, cover and simmer gently for 30 minutes until the lentils are tender and easy to crush.

3 Squeeze in the lemon juice, season with salt and pepper to taste. Ladle into warm bowls and serve.

Hot and sour
chicken and mushroom soup

Delicious hot and sour soups are all the rage at the moment. My recipe below is made with chicken, but you could also try making it with prawns, diced or minced pork, or just extra vegetables. Look out for frozen wontons and fish wontons in oriental stores or good supermarkets – the wontons make a great addition to the soup. Or serve the soup with Sesame Prawn Toasts (page 116).

PREPARATION: 10 minutes COOKING TIME: 15 minutes

SERVES 2

1 lemon grass stalk

600 ml (1 pint) hot chicken stock

4 boneless, skinless chicken thighs, diced

1–2 teaspoons Thai red curry paste

1 shallot, finely chopped

100 g (4 oz) shiitake mushrooms, sliced, or canned straw mushrooms, halved

2 teaspoons light muscovado sugar

2 teaspoons fish sauce

juice of 1 lemon

salt and freshly ground black pepper

1 salad onion, thinly sliced

1 red chilli, thinly sliced

handful of fresh coriander leaves

METHOD

1 Flatten the lemon grass stalk with a rolling pin or meat mallet and place in a pan with the chicken stock, chicken, curry paste and shallot; bring to the boil.

2 Add the mushrooms to the pan and simmer gently for 8–10 minutes.

3 Stir the sugar and fish sauce into the soup and simmer for 3 minutes until the chicken is cooked. Squeeze in the lemon juice and season to taste.

4 Ladle the soup into bowls and scatter over the salad onion, chilli and coriander. Serve immediately.

TRY THIS: If any of my family are feeling a bit off colour, I throw lots of shredded root ginger into the broth for a really soothing soup – especially good for coughs and colds.

Curried mussel soup

No, really, try it – it's fantastic, especially with the Green Onion Chapatis (page 121) or Tabletop Naan with Spicy Fried Onions (page 120).

PREPARATION: 20 minutes COOKING TIME: 20 minutes

SERVES 4

pinch of saffron strands

450 ml (¾ pint) hot vegetable stock

2 kg (4½ lb) fresh, live mussels, cleaned

150 ml (¼ pint) dry white wine

knob of butter

1 shallot, finely chopped

2 garlic cloves, peeled and finely chopped

1 small hot chilli, seeded and finely chopped

2 cm (¾ inch) piece fresh root ginger, finely chopped

½ teaspoon ground turmeric

½ teaspoon garam masala

150 ml carton double cream

juice of ½ lime

salt and freshly ground black pepper

1 tablespoon chopped fresh dill

METHOD

1 Place the saffron in a heatproof bowl and pour over the hot stock; set aside to infuse.

2 Place the mussels in a large pan and pour over the wine. Cover with a tight-fitting lid and cook for 5 minutes or so, shaking the pan occasionally until the shells open.

3 Strain the mussel liquid into a clean bowl.

4 Heat the butter in a large pan and gently cook the shallot, garlic, chilli and ginger until softened and golden. Add the spices, saffron stock and mussel liquid and simmer gently for 10 minutes.

5 Shell the mussels, saving about 20 to garnish and discarding any that don't open.

6 Stir the mussels and cream into the pan, add a squeeze of lime juice and season to taste. Warm through gently, stir in the dill, then ladle into bowls.

7 Divide the reserved mussels between the bowls and serve.

Rapido French onion soup and cheese croûtes

Simple but stylish, this version of the French classic is just right for a light lunch and takes minutes to make.

PREPARATION: 15 minutes   COOKING TIME: 40 minutes

SERVES 2

50 g (2 oz) butter

3 large Spanish onions, sliced

1 tablespoon caster sugar

2 garlic cloves, crushed

150 ml (¼ pint) dry white wine

600 ml (1 pint) hot, fresh chicken or vegetable stock

1 tablespoon Worcestershire sauce

1 small baguette

100 g (4 oz) Gruyère, finely grated

1 tablespoon French brandy (optional but dee-lish)

salt and freshly ground black pepper

METHOD

1 Melt the butter in a large pan and add the sliced onions. Sprinkle in the sugar and cook over a high heat for 10–15 minutes, stirring frequently until you get a lovely caramel brown tinge to your onions. Add the garlic and cook for a further 30 seconds.

2 Pour the wine into the pan and cook vigorously for 1–2 minutes. Stir in the hot stock and Worcestershire sauce, bring to the boil, reduce the heat and simmer for 15–20 minutes until the onions are tender.

3 Pre-heat the grill to high. Cut four diagonal slices of baguette and toast for 1–2 minutes on each side. Reduce the grill heat to medium.

4 Pile the cheese on top of the toasts. Return to the grill and cook until bubbling and golden.

5 If using the brandy, stir it into the soup, and season to taste. Then, using a slotted spoon, divide the onions between two soup bowls. Place the cheese croûtes on top of the onions, then ladle over the hot soup.

TRY THIS: There are lots of different ways to avoid your eyes watering when chopping onions, for example, wearing glasses, chewing parsley or chilling your onions before slicing them.

Rapido French onion soup and cheese croûtes

Succulent seafood
and roasted vegetable soup

This is a delicious, piquant soup full of flavour and packed with tender pieces of seafood. You'll need to use the oven as well as the hob, but the end result is well worth the effort. It's a great supper when paired with chunks of crusty bread.

PREPARATION: 15 minutes COOKING TIME: 50 minutes

SERVES 6

2 red peppers, seeded and quartered

1 aubergine, quartered

4 tablespoons olive oil

sea salt and freshly ground black pepper

1 large onion, chopped

2 celery stalks, chopped

4 garlic cloves, finely chopped

½ teaspoon chilli powder

50 g (2 oz) plain flour

1.2 litres (2 pints) hot fish stock

300 ml (½ pint) creamed tomatoes or passata

2 sprigs fresh thyme

1 teaspoon caster sugar

250 g (9 oz) fillet haddock or cod, cut into 2.5 cm (1 inch) chunks

250 g (9 oz) raw tiger prawns

250 g (9 oz) squid rings

juice of 1 lime

2 tablespoons chopped fresh parsley

METHOD

1 Pre-heat the oven to 200°C/400°F/Gas 6. Place the peppers and aubergine in a roasting tin. Drizzle over half the olive oil, season and roast for 25 minutes until tender and a little charred.

2 Heat the remaining oil in a large pan and cook the onion, celery and garlic for about 5 minutes. Add the chilli and flour and cook for 1 minute, stirring constantly. Gradually add the stock, then the tomatoes.

3 Cut the peppers and aubergine into 2.5 cm (1 inch) chunks and add to the pan with the thyme and sugar. Bring to the boil, cover and simmer for 15 minutes.

4 Add the seafood to the pan and simmer for a further 4–5 minutes until tender. Add lime juice, salt and pepper to taste. Stir in the parsley, ladle into bowls and serve with crusty bread and chilled white wine.

Spinach, mint
and garlic soup

It may be simple, but this soup is really bursting with fresh flavour. I like to top it with crunchy pieces of fried bacon, but leave them out and you've got a vegetarian-friendly bowlful.

PREPARATION: 15 minutes COOKING TIME: 30 minutes

SERVES 4

2 tablespoons olive oil

2 large white onions, roughly chopped

2 garlic cloves, roughly chopped

1 red chilli, finely chopped

1 bunch fresh mint, roughly chopped

1 bunch fresh parsley or coriander, roughly chopped

1.2 litres (2 pints) hot vegetable stock

75 g (3 oz) cubed pancetta or lardons

500 g (1 lb 2 oz) fresh young spinach, roughly chopped

juice of 1–2 lemons

salt and freshly ground black pepper

METHOD

1 Heat the oil in a large pan and cook the onions, garlic and chilli for 10 minutes until softened and golden. Add the herbs and stock, bring to the boil and simmer for 15 minutes.

2 Meanwhile, cook the bacon in a non-stick frying-pan until crisp and nicely browned. Drain on kitchen paper.

3 Add the spinach to the onion mixture and cook for 2 minutes. Add lemon juice, and salt and pepper to taste. Using a hand-blender, whizz the soup to a coarse purée. Ladle into bowls, scatter over the crispy bacon and a good grinding of black pepper, and serve with crusty bread.

CHEF'S TIP: Don't make this soup too far ahead of time – although it would still taste great, its lovely bright green colour would begin to fade.

Newfoundland
crab chowder

If you've never made chowder, this is the perfect place to start as it's so very easy. The potato base makes it a truly hearty soup, so you could easily serve it as a casual main meal. Canned crab is a great addition to this dish, but I've also made it with cubes of smoked fish, such as haddock, or large, juicy prawns. So go on, have a go – you won't be disappointed.

PREPARATION: 10 minutes COOKING TIME: 35 minutes

SERVES 4

25 g (1 oz) butter

4 rashers smoked streaky bacon, roughly chopped

2 shallots, finely chopped

450 g (1 lb) floury potatoes, diced

2 thyme sprigs

1 bay leaf

1.2 litres (2 pints) fish stock

2 x 170 g cans crabmeat, drained

200 g carton crème fraîche

4 tablespoons chopped fresh parsley

salt and freshly ground black pepper

METHOD

1 Melt the butter in a large pan and cook the bacon, shallots and potatoes for 4–5 minutes. Add the thyme, bay leaf and fish stock, bring to the boil and simmer for 25–30 minutes.

2 Stir the crabmeat and crème fraîche into the pan and heat through gently. Stir in the parsley and season to taste. Ladle into bowls and serve.

TRY THIS: In Newfoundland they always crumble crackers into their chowder at the table, and I find this a really good way to serve it – just scrunch them in your hand and scatter over the top of your soup immediately before you eat it.

Pacific prawn fu-yung

'Fu-yung' just means a Chinese egg dish. Here, to go with the prawns, I like to add a bit of shredded Chinese pork or sausage, or you can always throw in a bit of shredded ham if you like. Serve with a dollop of my Easy Mint Chutney (page 139) or Sweet Chilli Sauce (page 147).

PREPARATION: 15 minutes COOKING TIME: 10 minutes

SERVES 4

6 eggs

100 ml (3½ fl oz) chicken stock

2 tablespoons vegetable oil

4 salad onions, thinly sliced

1 red chilli, seeded and finely chopped

75 g (3 oz) shiitake mushrooms, thinly sliced

175 g (6 oz) cooked peeled prawns

100 g (4 oz) pork or ham, shredded

75 g (3 oz) beansprouts

1 tablespoon soy sauce

handful of fresh coriander leaves

METHOD

1 Beat together the eggs and stock until well blended.

2 Heat the oil in a large frying-pan and stir-fry the salad onions, chilli and mushrooms over a medium heat until beginning to soften.

3 Add the prawns, pork or ham and beansprouts, cook for 30 seconds, then add the soy sauce and coriander.

4 Pour over the beaten egg mixture and cook gently, stirring, until the egg is just set; serve immediately.

Deep-fried cod
in beer batter

Yes, this is a proper tasty batter to coat a nice piece of cod. It's the air in the beer that gives the batter a good crunchy finish, so, unlike other batters, don't rest this one – use it as soon as it's ready. Try to choose a high-quality beer with a malty flavour for a really great batter. Deep-fry until crisp and golden, and serve with my Perfect Golden, Crispy Chips (page 115) and Minted Mushy Chip-shop Peas (page 129) or Real Tartare Sauce (page 141).

PREPARATION: 5 minutes COOKING TIME: 20 minutes

SERVES 4

4 x 175 g (6 oz) pieces of cod

salt and freshly ground black pepper

200 g (7 oz) plain flour, plus extra for dusting

½ teaspoon salt

1 egg, beaten

330 ml bottle of beer

vegetable oil, for deep-frying

lemon wedges, to garnish

METHOD

1 Lightly season the fish and dust with flour.

2 Sift the flour and salt into a large bowl. Make a well in the centre, crack in the egg and gradually add the beer, stirring continuously, to make a smooth, frothy batter.

3 Dip the fish in the batter, making sure it is well covered, and shake off any excess. Deep-fry in hot oil for 4–5 minutes until crisp and golden. Drain on kitchen paper and serve hot, garnished with the lemon wedges.

TRY THIS: This quantity of batter is more than enough for four pieces of fish, so why not try dipping a few extras, such as red onion rings, to serve on the side?

Classic family fish cakes

These crisp-crumb fish cakes are a real family classic. I like to serve them with my Real Tartare Sauce (page 141) and a leafy salad such as the Rocket and Roast Onion Salad (page 124), or push the boat out and go for Perfect Golden, Crispy Chips (page 115) and Minted Mushy Chip-shop Peas (page 129).

PREPARATION: 25 minutes COOKING TIME: 15 minutes

SERVES 4

450 g (1 lb) floury potatoes, cubed

450 g (1 lb) smoked haddock

1 hard-boiled egg, chopped

2 tablespoons snipped chives or chopped fresh parsley

salt and freshly ground black pepper

2 tablespoons seasoned flour

1 egg, beaten

100 g (4 oz) white breadcrumbs

vegetable oil, for shallow-frying

METHOD

1 Cook the potatoes in a pan of boiling, salted water until tender. Drain and mash well.

2 Meanwhile, place the fish in a sauté-pan or frying-pan and cover with boiling water. Bring to the boil and simmer for 5 minutes until just cooked.

3 Drain the fish and remove the skin. Using a fork, flake the fish, discarding any bones. Mix together the potatoes, fish, boiled egg, chives and salt and pepper. Use your hands to shape the mixture into 4 or 8 even-sized round or triangular cakes.

4 Dust the fish cakes with the seasoned flour, dip in the beaten egg, then coat in the breadcrumbs, making sure they are completely covered.

5 Heat the oil in a frying-pan and shallow-fry for 3–4 minutes on each side until crisp and golden. Serve warm.

Classic family fish cakes *with* Real tartare sauce

Golden crumb-crunch scampi

Scampi is actually the tail of the langoustine, which is also known as the Dublin Bay prawn. These can be quite hard to find, and can also be quite pricey, so I often find it easier to make mine using fresh tiger prawns – though if you can get hold of the real thing, do give it a go. Because of the lovely fresh taste of the prawns, I prefer to keep this dish really simple and serve the scampi with a good dollop of my home-made Real Tartare Sauce (page 141) and a simple mixed salad made from lettuce, cucumber and tomatoes.

PREPARATION: 10 minutes COOKING TIME: 10 minutes

SERVES 4

vegetable oil, for deep-frying

32 large, raw tiger prawns, shelled

4 tablespoons seasoned flour

2 beaten eggs

75 g (3 oz) natural dried breadcrumbs

sea salt

lemon wedges and tartare sauce, to serve

METHOD

1 Heat about 6 cm (2½ inches) of vegetable oil in a wok or deep frying-pan.

2 Toss the prawns first in the seasoned flour, then the beaten egg. Give them a good shake to remove excess egg, then finally toss in the breadcrumbs. Deep-fry in batches for 2–3 minutes until golden brown and cooked through. Drain on kitchen paper and serve immediately.

TRY THIS: It's really important to use dried breadcrumbs for this dish as the crunchy coating is a lovely contrast to the juicy interior. I find supermarket breadcrumbs work very well, but if you have any stale white sliced bread, arrange it on a tray and leave to dry out completely. Once hard and dry, whizz in a food processor to form fine crumbs, then store in an airtight jar until ready to use.

Ocean cheese and potato pie

This is a fabulous twist on a classic family dish. It's great for after-work suppers because you can prepare the mash and the fish filling the day before. When you're ready to eat, spoon the mash over the fish mixture and pop it in the oven for 20 minutes. Sprinkle over the cheese and finish it off as described in step 5 below.

PREPARATION: 15 minutes COOKING TIME: 20 minutes

SERVES 4

1 kg (2¼ lb) floury potatoes, cubed

450 ml (¾ pint) milk

250 g (9 oz) smoked haddock

50 g (2 oz) butter

25 g (1 oz) plain flour

200 g (7 oz) Cheddar, grated

4 tablespoons fromage frais

150 g (5 oz) frozen peas

200 g (7 oz) large, cooked, peeled prawns

2 tablespoons snipped chives

salt and freshly ground black pepper

METHOD

1 Cook the potatoes in a large pan of boiling, salted water until tender.

2 Heat the milk in a frying-pan, add the haddock and poach for 5 minutes or so until just cooked. Transfer the fish to a plate and leave to cool. Do not discard the poaching milk.

3 Melt half the butter in a pan and stir in the flour. Cook gently for 1 minute, stirring continuously. Gradually add the poaching milk, stirring to make a smooth sauce. Bring to the boil, then remove from the heat and stir in three-quarters of the grated cheese, plus the fromage frais, peas, prawns and chives.

4 Flake in the fish, discarding the skin and any bones, and season to taste. Transfer to a heatproof dish.

5 Pre-heat the grill to medium. Drain the potatoes, mash well with the remaining butter and season to taste. Spoon the mash over the fish mixture and scatter the reserved cheese on top. Grind over some black pepper, then cook under the grill for 3–4 minutes until the top is golden. Serve warm.

Prawn and peanut pan-fried udon

Udon noodles are those lovely, thick white noodles you can buy now. A lot of supermarkets stock fresh ones, which are vacuum packed, so they have a long shelf life. If you have trouble finding them, use regular Chinese-style egg noodles.

PREPARATION: 15 minutes COOKING TIME: 15 minutes

SERVES 4

300 g (11 oz) dried udon noodles or 500 g (1 lb 2 oz) fresh

vegetable oil, for frying

4 shallots, very finely sliced

2 large red chillies, seeded and thinly sliced

2 teaspoons sesame oil

300 g (11 oz) large, cooked, peeled prawns

200 g (7 oz) fresh beansprouts

handful of fresh coriander leaves

2 fresh limes, cut into wedges, for serving

FOR THE PEANUT SAUCE

200 g (7 oz) salted roasted peanuts

2 garlic cloves, peeled

2.5 cm (1 inch) piece root ginger, peeled and roughly chopped

200 ml carton coconut cream

1 tablespoon soy sauce

1 teaspoon hot chilli sauce

METHOD

1 Plunge the noodles into a large pan of boiling water. Bring back to the boil, simmer for 1 minute until tender, then drain well. Cool under cold water.

2 Make the sauce: place the peanuts, garlic and ginger in a food processor and whizz until finely chopped. Transfer to a bowl and stir in the coconut cream; add soy and chilli sauces, to taste.

3 Heat 1 cm (½ inch) of vegetable oil in a wok or large frying-pan. When the oil is very hot, add the shallots and chillies and cook for 3–4 minutes until crisp and golden brown. Drain on kitchen paper.

4 Pour most of the oil out of the wok, leaving just a thin coating, then add the sesame oil. Cook the noodles for 1–2 minutes, then stir in the prawns and peanut sauce; stir in enough water (200–300 ml/ 7–10 fl oz) – to make a thick, glossy sauce and cook for 3–4 minutes until piping hot.

5 Stir in the beansprouts and coriander. Divide between plates and scatter over the crispy shallot mixture. Serve with wedges of lime for squeezing over.

Devilled, dusted whitebait

This is a traditional pub dish – truly delicious. Serve unadorned as a starter, or make it a main course by serving it with some lovely crusty bread and a crisp green salad – you can't go wrong.

PREPARATION: 5 minutes   COOKING TIME: 5 minutes

SERVES 4

375 g (13 oz) whitebait, thawed if frozen

25 g (1 oz) plain flour

½ teaspoon salt

1 teaspoon English mustard powder

½ teaspoon cayenne pepper, plus extra for dusting

½ teaspoon paprika

finely grated rind of 1 lemon

vegetable oil, for deep-frying

lemon wedges and herb sprigs, to serve

METHOD

1 Rinse the whitebait and pat dry with kitchen paper.

2 Place the flour, salt, mustard, cayenne, paprika and lemon rind in a polythene bag. Add the whitebait and shake well to coat.

3 Deep-fry the whitebait in hot oil for 2 minutes until golden. Drain on kitchen paper. Transfer to a serving platter and dust with a little cayenne. Garnish with lemon wedges and herb sprigs and serve immediately.

Classic moules marinière

This French classic is really easy to make, and when mussels are in season – September to April – they're cheap and plentiful. Serve with salad, crusty bread and a glass of your favourite chilled white wine – ooh la la!

PREPARATION: 10 minutes COOKING TIME: 15 minutes

SERVES 4

25 g (1 oz) butter

1 onion, chopped

2 garlic cloves, finely chopped

150 ml (¼ pint) dry white wine

150 ml (¼ pint) fish stock

2 kg (4½ lb) live, clean mussels

3 tablespoons double cream

2 tablespoons chopped fresh parsley

salt and freshly ground black pepper

METHOD

1 Melt the butter in a large pan and cook the onion and garlic for 3–4 minutes until softened and golden. Then pour in the wine, bring to the boil and add the mussels.

2 Cover and cook over a high heat for 4–5 minutes until all the shells have opened. Transfer the mussels to a serving dish, discarding any that remain closed, leaving the juices behind.

3 Add the fish stock to the juices, bring to the boil, then reduce the heat. Stir the cream and parsley into the pan juices, add pepper and check for salt. Ladle the pan juices over the mussels and serve hot.

Roasted
lemon bay garlic cod

This is a really light dish – I've simply marinated the fish with a little garlic and parsley, and cooked it over bay and lemon so it picks up the fragrance. Serve with a leafy salad or my New Millennium Posh Potato Salad (page 133) or Mozzamary Garlic Bread (page 122) and a good bottle of Chardonnay for a lovely lunch.

PREPARATION: 10 minutes + 10 minutes marinating COOKING TIME: 10 minutes

SERVES 4

4 garlic cloves, crushed

1 tablespoon chopped fresh parsley

2 tablespoons olive oil

salt and freshly ground black pepper

4 x 150 g (5 oz) cod fillets

2 lemons, thinly sliced

10 fresh bay leaves

METHOD

1 Preheat the oven to 220°C/425°F/Gas 7. Mix together the garlic, parsley, olive oil and some salt and pepper. Rub the mixture over the fish fillets and set aside for 10 minutes or so.

2 Arrange the lemons and bay leaves on a baking sheet and sit the cod fillets on top. Cook in the hot oven for 8–10 minutes until just cooked and a little charred. Serve immediately.

Roasted lemon bay garlic cod *with* Warm sweet potato and roast tomato cheese salad

Lobster
and papaya salad

Here's a touch of luxury when you're feeling a bit flash. Ask the fishmonger to halve the lobster and remove all the meat for you – alternatively, you can buy lobster ready prepared in supermarkets. Serve with warm baby new potatoes in their skins for an exquisite main course, or how about my New Millennium Posh Potato Salad (page 133)?

PREPARATION: 10 minutes

SERVES 2

1 kg (2¼ lb) lobster, cooked and shelled

60 g bag baby salad leaves

1 papaya, skinned, seeded and sliced

1 avocado, skinned, stoned and sliced

1 tablespoon raspberry vinegar

2 tablespoons olive oil

salt and freshly ground black pepper

chervil or dill sprigs, to garnish

METHOD

1 Cut the lobster meat into 2 cm (¾ inch) slices or chunks.

2 Divide the salad leaves between 2 large plates and arrange the papaya and avocado slices on top of the leaves. Add the lobster meat.

3 Whisk together the vinegar, olive oil and some salt and pepper, then drizzle over the salad.

4 Garnish with herb sprigs and serve.

Crispy cache calamari

Memories of Mediterranean holidays come flooding back, as there's nothing like a plateful of crispy calamari and a glass of dry white wine to make you enjoy the summer – also fantastic for a weekend lunch in the garden. I use a very simple egg-free batter for a really crisp result that's heavenly to eat. I only wish the sun would shine! I like to serve it tapas style, with Jacqueline's Potato Skins with Guacamole (page 110), a fresh tomato salad and some juicy black olives.

PREPARATION: 10 minutes COOKING TIME: 10 minutes

SERVES 4

175 g (6 oz) self-raising flour

1 teaspoon paprika, plus extra for dusting

½ teaspoon salt

450 g (1 lb) cleaned fresh squid cut into 1 cm (½ inch) wide rings

4 tablespoons seasoned flour, for dusting

vegetable oil, for deep-frying

cayenne pepper (optional) and lemon and lime wedges, to garnish

METHOD

1 Sift the flour, paprika and salt into a bowl. Gradually beat in 250 ml (8 fl oz) water to make a smooth batter.

2 Dust the squid in the seasoned flour, then dip in the batter, shaking off any excess. Deep-fry for about 3–4 minutes until crisp and golden. Drain on kitchen paper.

3 Transfer the calamari to serving plates, dust with paprika or cayenne pepper, garnish with lemon and lime wedges and serve.

TRY THIS: The tentacles are just as tasty as the body of the squid. Make sure the 'beak' has been removed (check with your fishmonger: if you can't, it's the hard, crusty bit directly above the tentacles), then batter and fry as for the rings above.

Tuna burgers
with red onion salsa

A great recipe for meaty fish, such as tuna. I've added wasabi, which is Japanese horseradish, and it gives a fantastic kick to the fish, though you can add a dab of English mustard if you can't get hold of it. This stylish dish is a perfect starter for a dinner party, but makes a terrific main course supper if served with Grate Hash Browns (page 117) or chips (page 115).

PREPARATION: 25 minutes COOKING TIME: 10 minutes

SERVES 4

FOR THE SALSA

1 red onion, finely diced

2 plum tomatoes, seeded and finely chopped

1 green chilli, seeded and finely chopped

juice of 1 lime

1 tablespoon olive oil

salt and freshly ground black pepper

FOR THE BURGERS

400 g (14 oz) fresh tuna

1–2 teaspoons wasabi paste

1 tablespoon sesame seeds

salt and freshly ground black pepper

1 tablespoon seasoned flour

vegetable oil, for shallow-frying

1 ciabatta loaf, sliced and toasted

METHOD

1 Begin by making the salsa: stir all the ingredients together, and set aside at room temperature for at least an hour.

2 Place the tuna in a food processor and pulse until coarsely minced. Mix with the wasabi paste, sesame seeds and some salt and pepper. With damp hands, shape the mixture into 4 even-sized burgers.

3 Dust the burgers in the seasoned flour, shaking off any excess. Shallow-fry for 2–4 minutes on each side until golden brown and just cooked through. Be careful not to overcook them or they'll quickly become dry.

4 Place the tuna burgers on the toasted ciabatta and top with a dollop of the salsa. Garnish with slices of fresh lime and serve warm.

Peppy's barbecue chicken
with Jamaican fried dumplings

The herby fried dumplings are the perfect accompaniment to my mum's spicy barbecue chicken. For an extra kick, why not add a ¼ teaspoon of chilli flakes to the dumpling mixture and wash it down with a glass of my Sweet 'n' Easy Mango Lassi (page 170).

PREPARATION: 15 minutes + 20 minutes marinating COOKING TIME: 15 minutes

SERVES 4

4 tablespoons tomato ketchup

juice of 1 large lemon

2 tablespoons soy sauce

1 tablespoon dark brown sugar

½ teaspoon ground allspice (Jamaican pepper)

½ teaspoon cayenne pepper

½ teaspoon salt

4 skinless, boneless chicken breasts

FOR THE FRIED DUMPLINGS

200 g (7 oz) plain flour

1 teaspoon baking powder

2 tablespoons finely chopped parsley

½ teaspoon dried thyme

½ teaspoon salt

200 ml (7 fl oz) milk

vegetable oil, for deep-frying

METHOD

1 In a large bowl, mix together the ketchup, lemon juice, soy sauce, sugar, allspice, cayenne and salt. Add the chicken breasts, stirring to coat in the marinade, then cover and set aside for 20 minutes or so.

2 Meanwhile, make the dumplings: mix together the flour, baking powder, herbs and salt. Beat in the milk to make a thick batter.

3 Heat 5 cm (2 inches) of oil in a wok or deep frying-pan – the oil should be hot enough so that when a cube of bread is added to the pan, it browns in about 1½ minutes. Cook spoonfuls of the mixture, in batches, for 3–4 minutes until puffed, golden brown and cooked through. Drain on kitchen paper.

4 Cook the chicken on a hot barbecue or in an oiled griddle pan for 8–10 minutes on each side until well browned and cooked through. Serve with mixed salad leaves drizzled with olive oil and lemon juice.

Charred chicken and pepper fajitas

The sight and sound of sizzling chicken and crispy vegetables arriving at your table is a joy to behold, and it doesn't have to be in a restaurant: this can be achieved at home for a fraction of the cost.

PREPARATION: 15 minutes COOKING TIME: 10 minutes

SERVES 2

2 large skinless, boneless chicken breasts, cut into 1 cm (½ inch) wide strips

1 yellow pepper, cut lengthways into 1 cm (½ inch) wide strips

1 red onion, thickly sliced

½ teaspoon dried oregano

¼ teaspoon crushed chillies

2 tablespoons vegetable oil

grated rind and juice of 1 lime

salt and freshly ground black pepper

4 x 20 cm (8 inch) flour tortillas

sunflower oil, for brushing

leafy salad, to serve

150 ml carton soured cream

METHOD

1 Place the chicken strips, pepper, red onion, oregano, chillies, oil, lime rind and juice in a large bowl. Add plenty of seasoning and toss together until well mixed.

2 Heat a flat griddle or heavy non-stick frying-pan. Add the chicken mixture and cook over a high heat for 6–8 minutes, turning once or twice, until the mixture is well browned, lightly charred and cooked through.

3 Brush the tortillas with sunflower oil and briefly warm them in the microwave for 10 seconds, or heat them in a dry frying-pan for a few seconds on each side.

4 Serve separately, or pile the fajitas in the middle of your warm tortillas, add salad and a dollop of soured cream, roll up and enjoy. Serve with a bottle or two of chilled Mexican lager – *salud*!

Cheeky chicken tikka masala

Forget having to wait for your take-away chicken tikka: this is one of the easiest curries there is to make. If it's summer, why not have a go at cooking the chicken skewers over the old barbie?

PREPARATION: 20 minutes + 2 hours marinating COOKING TIME: 25 minutes

SERVES 4

4 skinless, boneless chicken breasts, cubed

2.5 cm (1 inch) piece root ginger, finely chopped

2 garlic cloves, finely chopped

1 teaspoon chilli powder

salt and freshly ground black pepper

2 tablespoons chopped fresh coriander

juice of 1 lime

2 tablespoons vegetable oil

1 onion, finely chopped

1 red chilli, seeded and finely chopped

1 teaspoon ground turmeric

300 ml carton double cream

juice of ½ lemon

Pulao Rice (page 126) or Tabletop Naan with Spicy Fried Onions (page 120), to serve

handful of fresh coriander leaves, to garnish

METHOD

1 Place the chicken breasts in a large bowl and mix with the ginger, garlic, chilli, salt, pepper, coriander, lime juice and 1 tablespoon of the oil. Set aside for 2 hours.

2 Pre-heat the grill to high. Thread the chicken on to skewers and cook under the grill for 12 minutes or so, turning frequently until well browned.

3 Meanwhile, heat the remaining oil in a large pan and cook the onion and chilli for 5–8 minutes until dark golden. Add the turmeric and cook for 30 seconds. Stir in the cream and cook gently for a couple of minutes.

4 Slide the chicken off the skewers and stir into the creamy sauce. Simmer for 5 minutes or so until the chicken is cooked through. Check the seasoning, adding some lemon juice to taste, and serve with rice or naan. Garnish with the coriander.

Cheeky chicken tikka masala *with* Green onion chapatis

Wok-it chicken chow mein

If you've got some roast chicken left over from last night's dinner, simply shred it up and make this lovely chicken chow mein – perfect for a quick supper. One of those packets of fresh stir-fry vegetables is great to have on stand-by for this.

PREPARATION: 10 minutes COOKING TIME: 15 minutes

SERVES 2

175 g (6 oz) egg noodles

1 tablespoon sunflower oil

1 onion, thinly sliced

2 garlic cloves, thinly sliced

1 cm (½ inch) piece root ginger, finely chopped (optional)

100 g (4 oz) beansprouts

100 g (4 oz) mangetout, halved lengthways, or peas

175 g (6 oz) cooked chicken, shredded

1 tablespoon soy sauce

1 tablespoon Sweet Chilli Sauce (page 147)

METHOD

1 Cook the noodles in a large pan of boiling, salted water according to the packet instructions.

2 Meanwhile, heat the oil in a wok and stir-fry the onion over a high heat for 2–3 minutes until beginning to brown. Add the garlic, ginger (if using), beansprouts and mangetout or peas and stir-fry for 1 minute.

3 Drain the noodles well and add to the wok with the chicken and soy sauce; cook for 2 minutes until piping hot. Stir in the sweet chilli sauce and serve immediately.

Wok-it chicken chow mein

Scrunchy
sweet and sour chicken

Chicken and pineapple is a wonderful combination, and this dish shows it off to great effect. It has a lovely fresh flavour that's sure to be popular with all the family. I like to serve it with Excellent Egg and Ginger Fried Rice (page 114).

PREPARATION: 20 minutes COOKING TIME: 15 minutes

SERVES 4

2 egg yolks

2 tablespoons cornflour

salt and freshly ground black pepper

4 skinless, boneless chicken breasts, cubed

vegetable oil, for deep-frying

FOR THE SWEET AND SOUR SAUCE

1 onion, sliced

1 small red pepper, cut into 2.5 cm (1 inch) pieces

1 small orange pepper, cut into 2.5 cm (1 inch) pieces

435 g can pineapple cubes in natural juice

1 tablespoon cornflour

2 tablespoons tomato ketchup

2 tablespoons light soy sauce

1 tablespoon white wine vinegar

handful of fresh coriander leaves, to garnish

METHOD

1 Mix together the egg yolks with a tablespoon of water, the cornflour and some salt and pepper.

2 Heat 5 cm (2 inches) of oil in a wok or deep frying-pan. Toss the chicken in the cornflour mixture and deep-fry in batches for 5 minutes or so until crisp and golden. Drain on kitchen paper.

3 Empty the oil from the wok to leave a thin coating in the pan. Stir-fry the onion and peppers over a high heat for 2–3 minutes. Strain the pineapple cubes (reserving the juice), add to the pan and cook for a minute or two.

4 Mix together the cornflour and a little of the pineapple juice to form a paste, then stir in the remaining juice, the ketchup, soy sauce, vinegar and 135 ml (4½ fl oz) water. Pour this into the pan and bring to the boil, stirring until the mixture thickens.

5 Stir the chicken pieces into the pan and simmer for 5 minutes until cooked through. Check the seasoning, then divide between bowls, scatter over the coriander and serve.

Scrunchy sweet and sour chicken *with* Excellent egg and ginger fried rice

Sticky maple syrup ribs

I love a sticky rib, and there's loads of different ways to marinate or glaze them. This is an easy and tasty way to get good results, and works well on the barbie too. Go easy on the chilli flakes if the kids are joining in. Try serving the ribs with Buttered Slam Jackets (page 106) and a side order of Citrus Couscous and Sultana Salad (page 134).

PREPARATION: 10 minutes COOKING TIME: 40 minutes

SERVES 4

2 tablespoons tomato purée

1 tablespoon cornflour

juice of 2 limes

2 tablespoons maple syrup

2 garlic cloves, crushed

½ teaspoon dried chilli flakes

½ teaspoon salt

750 g (1½ lb) pork ribs

METHOD

1 Mix together the tomato purée and cornflour to make a paste. Stir in the lime juice, maple syrup, garlic, chilli and salt.

2 Pre-heat the grill to medium. Rub the mixture into the pork ribs then arrange on a grill rack. Cook under the grill or on a barbecue for 30 minutes, turning occasionally, until well cooked and nicely browned. You can also cook them in the oven if you prefer: pre-heat the oven to 190°C/375°F/Gas 5, pop the ribs on a wire rack, place on a baking tray and cook for 35–45 minutes.

TRY THIS: This glaze is also very tasty on other cuts of pork, such as steaks or chops, but you will need to reduce the cooking time if the meat is boneless.

Crisp-crumbed pan pork escalopes

This is a favourite dish in my house as it's lovely straight from the pan– especially when accompanied by some lovely Breaking Bubble and Savoy Squeak (page 111) and grilled tomatoes. Any left-overs are great the next day, sandwiched between a couple of slices of crusty white bread and topped with a squirt of mayonnaise or a dash of brown sauce – salivating!

PREPARATION: 20 minutes COOKING TIME: 15 minutes

SERVES 4

500 g (1 lb 2 oz) pork fillet or boneless loin chops

2 garlic cloves, crushed

1 tablespoon Dijon mustard

¼ teaspoon cayenne pepper or chilli powder

salt and freshly ground black pepper

100 g (4 oz) fresh white breadcrumbs

2 tablespoons freshly grated Parmesan

2 tablespoons seasoned flour

2 eggs, beaten

vegetable oil, for shallow-frying

lemon wedges, to serve

METHOD

1 If using pork fillet, cut into 2 cm (¾ inch) slices. Place a piece of sliced pork or a chop on a sheet of greaseproof paper or plastic wrap, cover with a second sheet and, using a rolling pin or meat mallet, flatten to a thickness of about 5 mm (¼ inch). Repeat for the remaining meat (or ask your butcher to do this for you).

2 Mix together the garlic, mustard, cayenne or chilli powder and a little salt and pepper and spread over the pork. Stir together the breadcrumbs and Parmesan.

3 Toss the pork in the seasoned flour, shaking off any excess, dip in the beaten egg and then into the cheesy breadcrumbs, to coat.

4 Heat the oil in a large frying-pan and shallow-fry in batches for 3 minutes on each side until golden brown and cooked through. Drain on kitchen paper and serve warm.

TRY THIS: This method also works very well with frying steak, chicken and turkey breasts.

Thai-style
yellow pork curry

If you like creamy, delicate curries, this is the one for you. To enhance the flavour, serve with plain boiled jasmine rice and a side order of Tabletop Naan (page 120) to help mop up all those lovely coconutty juices.

PREPARATION: 15 minutes COOKING TIME: 20 minutes

SERVES 4

2 tablespoons vegetable oil

2 salad onions, thinly sliced

1 garlic clove, thinly sliced

500 g (1 lb 2 oz) pork fillet, cubed

1 aubergine, cubed

400 ml can coconut milk

3 kaffir lime leaves, shredded

2 teaspoons yellow or green Thai curry paste

150 g (5 oz) shiitake mushrooms, sliced

220 g can sliced water chestnuts, drained

2 tablespoons light soy sauce

1 teaspoon fish sauce

handful fresh basil leaves

2 limes, cut into wedges

METHOD

1 Heat the oil in a large pan and cook the salad onions and garlic for 2 minutes. Add the pork and aubergine and stir-fry for 3–4 minutes until the pork turns creamy white.

2 Stir in the coconut milk, lime leaves and curry paste and simmer for 10 minutes.

3 Add the shiitake mushrooms and water chestnuts and cook for a further 5 minutes. Stir in the soy sauce, fish sauce and fresh basil leaves. Serve with plain rice and lime wedges for squeezing over.

Thai-style yellow pork curry

Gina's classic super shepherd's pie

You've seen it before, but you really can't beat an old classic, and this is one of my family's favourites. What's different is the addition of soy sauce and Tabasco for a real kick and guaranteed clean bowls. My neighbour Gina thinks it's *suuper*!

PREPARATION: 10 minutes COOKING TIME: 25 minutes

SERVES 2

450 g (1 lb) floury potatoes, diced

1 tablespoon vegetable oil

1 large carrot, diced

1 small onion, finely chopped

300 g (11 oz) minced lamb

300 ml (½ pint) hot lamb stock

1 tablespoon brown sauce

2 teaspoons soy sauce

2 tablespoons milk

knob of butter

1 teaspoon cornflour

75 g (3 oz) frozen peas

salt and freshly ground black pepper

few drops of Tabasco

100 g (4 oz) grated Cheddar – optional but nice

METHOD

1 Cook the potatoes in a large pan of boiling, salted water for 10–12 minutes until tender.

2 Meanwhile, heat the oil in a large frying-pan and cook the carrot and onion for about 1 minute over a medium–high heat, then add the lamb mince and stir-fry until well browned. Pour in the hot stock and stir in the brown sauce and soy sauce. Bring to the boil and simmer rapidly for 3–4 minutes.

3 Drain the potatoes well and return to the pan, mash well, then beat in the milk and butter until smooth and creamy.

4 Mix the cornflour and a little water to a paste, and stir into the lamb mixture with the peas; bring back to the boil, stirring, until slightly thickened. Season with salt, pepper and Tabasco, to taste.

5 Pre-heat the grill to medium. Spoon the mince mixture into a heatproof dish and top with the mashed potato. Using a fork, mark a criss-cross pattern on the top and sprinkle over the grated cheese. Place under the grill for 3 minutes until the pie is speckled with brown or lovely and golden if using cheese.

Granny's corned-beef hash and fried egg

This is wonderful comfort food that I first tasted when it was cooked by the granny of one of my mates. Obviously, garlic and Tabasco have been added by me for one reason – *taste*. No wonder we covered the original in ketchup – sorry, Gran. Serve with greens or bok choi stir-fried in sesame oil, a splash of soy sauce and a teaspoon of runny honey – yummy!

PREPARATION: 10 minutes COOKING TIME: 25 minutes

SERVES 2

350 g (12 oz) floury potatoes, peeled and diced

1–2 tablespoons vegetable oil

1 small onion, chopped

2 garlic cloves, crushed

200 g can corned beef

few shakes of Tabasco or other chilli sauce

2 eggs

knob of butter

salt and freshly ground black pepper

METHOD

1 Cook the potatoes in a large pan of boiling, salted water for 10–12 minutes until tender.

2 Meanwhile, heat the oil in a small frying-pan and cook the onion and garlic for about 5 minutes until softened.

3 Open the can of corned beef and turn out onto a chopping board. Chop roughly and add to the pan.

4 Drain the potatoes well and add to the corned beef mixture. Crush with a fork, stirring to combine the mixture. Cook for 5 minutes until a crust forms on the bottom. Add salt, pepper and a shake of Tabasco then break up the mixture.

5 Add more oil if necessary and continue to cook the mixture until the base is golden and crusty. Break up once more and leave to cook again until crusty underneath.

6 Meanwhile, heat a small frying-pan, add the knob of butter. When it's beginning to melt and foam break in the eggs and cook, preferably sunny side up. Divide the hash between two plates, slide an egg on top of each and serve with a glass of iced lemon barley water.

Lightning lamb dhansak

One of the most popular dishes on any Indian menu and absolutely delicious. For complete authenticity, it can take a whole day to make lamb dhansak, but this lightning version combines all the flavours and tastes superb. Tamarind paste is available in large supermarkets or good delis.

PREPARATION: 20 minutes COOKING TIME: 25 minutes

SERVES 4

500 g (1lb 2 oz) cubed lamb

2 tablespoons garam masala

2–3 tablespoons vegetable oil

2 onions, thinly sliced

2 garlic cloves, thinly sliced

200 g (7 oz) diced pumpkin or squash

100 g (4 oz) red lentils

600 ml (1 pint) hot vegetable stock

1 tablespoon curry paste

1 tablespoon tamarind paste

25 g (1 oz) caster sugar

salt and freshly ground black pepper

2 tablespoons chopped fresh mint or coriander

juice of 1 lemon

Pulao Rice (page 126), to serve

METHOD

1 Toss the lamb in the garam masala. Heat 1 tablespoon of the oil in a large pan and quickly brown the lamb. Transfer to a plate and set aside.

2 Add a little more oil to the pan, then cook the onions, garlic and pumpkin or squash for 5 minutes until softened and beginning to brown.

3 Now add the lentils, stock, curry paste, tamarind paste and sugar and return the lamb to the pan. Bring to the boil, cover and simmer for 25–30 minutes, stirring occasionally, until the mixture is thickened and the ingredients are lovely and tender.

4 Check the seasoning, then stir in the mint or coriander and lemon juice, to taste. Serve with pulao rice.

TRY THIS: Use the remaining squash (or pumpkin) to make the Butternut Squash Spiced Soup on page 48.

Lightning lamb dhansak *with* Pulao rice

Café chilli beef tacos

This is a fantastic chilli with a really developed flavour, which it gets from my secret ingredient – coffee! Try it, it really packs a punch. By serving with Buttered Slam Jackets (page 106), you'll have a fast main meal to die for.

PREPARATION: 10 minutes COOKING TIME: 30 minutes

SERVES 4

1 tablespoon vegetable oil

1 onion, finely chopped

2 garlic cloves, finely chopped

2 red chillies, seeded and finely chopped

500 g (1 lb 2 oz) minced beef

1 teaspoon Chinese five-spice powder

400 g can kidney beans, drained

400 g can chopped tomatoes

150 ml (¼ pint) strong black coffee

salt and freshly ground black pepper

8 taco shells

shredded lettuce plus soured cream and paprika, to serve

METHOD

1 Heat the oil in a large pan and cook the onion, garlic and chillies for 3–4 minutes until beginning to soften. Add the mince and five-spice powder and cook for a further 3–4 minutes, stirring, until the meat begins to brown.

2 Add the kidney beans, tomatoes and coffee. Bring to the boil and simmer for 20 minutes until the mixture is thick and fairly dark. Season to taste.

3 Fill the taco shells with shredded lettuce, then pile in the chilli mixture. Top with a spoonful of soured cream and a shake of paprika and serve. A glass of chilled Mexican lager is always a winner with this recipe.

Café chilli beef tacos

Pappardelle
with chilli caper oil and baby mozzarella

For a light, versatile and fun meal this is a real winner. The combination of wonderful strong flavours with the delicate taste and texture of mozzarella blends beautifully. Great as a starter for those impromptu suppers, or simply increase the quantities and serve as a main course. Strips of Parma ham draped on top would be a lovely addition.

PREPARATION: 15 minutes COOKING TIME: 10 minutes

SERVES 4

250 g (9 oz) pasta ribbons, such as pappardelle, fettucine or lasagnette

3 tablespoons olive oil

large handful fresh basil leaves

2 garlic cloves, thinly sliced

1 red chilli, thinly sliced

2 tablespoons pickled capers, well rinsed and dried

juice of 1 lime

sea salt and freshly ground black pepper

150 g (15 oz) bocconcini (baby mozzarella), halved, or ball mozzarella, diced

METHOD

1 Cook the pasta in a large pan of boiling, salted water according to the packet instructions.

2 Two minutes before the pasta is ready, heat the oil in a frying-pan and cook the basil, garlic, chilli and capers for 2 minutes. Squeeze in the lime juice and check the seasoning.

3 Drain the pasta well and return to the pan. Toss with the infused oil mixture and the mozzarella. Divide between 4 bowls and serve with a good grinding of black pepper.

Deep-pan American-style cheese-ring pizza crust

This is one of those thick pizzas that has the cheese inside the ring crust. It's a little more complicated than other pizzas, so if you don't want to bother making a cheese ring, simply scatter the cheese over the top.

PREPARATION: 25 minutes + 1 hour resting COOKING TIME: 20 minutes

SERVES 4

350 g (12 oz) strong white flour

1 teaspoon table salt

7 g sachet easy blend yeast

2 tablespoons olive oil

250 ml (8 fl oz) warm water

FOR THE TOPPING AND CRUST

150 g ball mozzarella, drained

2 tablespoons chopped fresh parsley

1 garlic clove, crushed

salt and freshly ground black pepper

100 ml (3½ fl oz) passata

2 tomatoes, thinly sliced

75 g (3 oz) thinly sliced pepperoni

4 green pickled chillies, sliced

METHOD

1 Place the flour, salt and yeast in a food processor fitted with a dough hook. With the motor running, pour in the oil and warm water and mix to form a soft, stretchy dough. Alternatively, make the dough by hand and knead on a floured board for 5 minutes.

2 Transfer the dough to a bowl, rub the surface with a little oil and cover with a clean, damp tea towel. Set aside at room temperature for an hour or so until the dough has roughly doubled in size. Meanwhile, roughly chop the mozzarella and mix with the parsley, garlic and some seasoning.

3 Pre-heat the oven to 230°C/450°F/Gas 8. On a floured surface, roll the dough into a thin 40 cm (16 inch) circle. Arrange the cheese around the edge of the dough, leaving a 4 cm (1½ inch) border. Dampen the inner edge of the cheese ring, then pull the outer edge over to cover the cheese. Press down firmly to seal.

4 Carefully turn the pizza on to a large baking sheet so the joins are underneath. Spoon the passata within the border, then scatter over the toppings. Bake for 12–15 minutes until browned and crisp. Cut into wedges and serve immediately with a lovely crisp, green salad sprinkled with olive oil and balsamic vinegar.

Prawn and Parma pizzinis

These delightful pizzinis are a great brunch treat, or are ideal as a light snack or starter. You could also serve them with Grate Hash Browns (page 117) for a tasty family dinner – the kids love 'em too.

PREPARATION: 15 minutes COOKING TIME: 35 minutes

SERVES 4

150 g pack pizza-base mix

1 tablespoon olive oil

flour, for kneading

FOR THE TOMATO SAUCE

250 g (9 oz) ripe tomatoes, seeded and roughly chopped

2 garlic cloves, finely chopped

4 thyme sprigs

1 tablespoon tomato purée

1 tablespoon olive oil

salt and freshly ground black pepper

FOR THE TOPPING

200 g (7 oz) large cooked peeled prawns

4 slices Parma ham, halved lengthways

handful of fresh basil leaves

fresh Parmesan, to serve

METHOD

1 Pre-heat the oven to 220°C/425°F/Gas 7. Place the pizza-base mix in a large bowl and stir in the olive oil and enough warm water (about 120 ml/4 fl oz) to make a soft dough. Knead vigorously on a lightly floured surface for about 5 minutes until smooth and elastic.

2 Break the dough into 4 even pieces, then pat out between the hands to make rough 12 cm (4½ inch) circles. Transfer to a large baking sheet and set aside in a warm place for 10 minutes or so to rise.

3 Make the tomato sauce: place the tomatoes, garlic, thyme, tomato purée and olive oil in a small pan. Simmer over a medium to high heat for 10–20 minutes, stirring occasionally until thickened and pulpy. Season to taste.

4 Spoon the sauce on to the dough circles, then scatter over the prawns. Ripple the strips of Parma ham across the top, then bake for 10 minutes until the pizza bases have risen and set. Slip the pizzinis off the baking sheet and continue to cook directly on the oven rack for a further 5 minutes until the bases are crisp and golden. Scatter a few basil leaves and some shavings of Parmesan over each pizzini and serve.

Prawn and Parma pizzinis

Tasty tuna pan-fried pizza

This pizza requires no proving, as I use a scone-style base that you can fry in the pan. It's quick, simple and very tasty. Don't forget, anything goes, so just change the topping to suit the contents of your fridge and store-cupboard.

PREPARATION: 15 minutes COOKING TIME: 20 minutes

SERVES 2

FOR THE TOMATO SAUCE

1 tablespoon olive oil

2 garlic cloves, finely chopped

2 salad onions, finely chopped

200 g can chopped tomatoes

handful of fresh basil, roughly torn

1 tablespoon tomato ketchup

salt and freshly ground black pepper

FOR THE TOPPING

200 g can tuna in olive oil, drained and flaked into chunks

1 red onion, thinly sliced

75 g (3 oz) black olives

75 g (3 oz) mozzarella or Cheddar, diced

FOR THE DOUGH

225 g (8 oz) self-raising flour

pinch of salt

2 tablespoons freshly grated Parmesan

150 ml (¼ pint) warm water

2 tablespoons olive oil, plus extra for drizzling

METHOD

1 Heat the oil in a small pan and cook the garlic and onions for 2–3 minutes until softened. Stir in the tomatoes, basil, ketchup and a little seasoning. Bring to the boil and simmer for 5–10 minutes until pulpy.

2 Sift the flour and salt into a large bowl, then stir in the cheese. Make a well in the centre and pour in the water and 1 tablespoon of olive oil. Mix into a soft dough, then roll out into a 25 cm (10 inch) circle.

3 Heat 1 tablespoon of olive oil in a 25 cm (10 inch) skillet and cook the dough for 5–6 minutes until the underside is golden brown. While the dough is cooking, spoon over the tomato sauce and scatter over the topping ingredients. Drizzle over a little olive oil and place under a preheated grill for 3–4 minutes until the top is golden and the base is cooked through. Cut into wedges and serve with lots of leafy salad.

Premier pistou-pasta

You know what it's like: late in from work or fancy a quick lunch, well…a touch of French pistou blended with some al dente Italian pasta and you have the perfect answer on a plate that's refreshingly tasty and healthy. Some Rocket and Roast Onion Salad (page 124) served on the side would be a perfect addition.

PREPARATION: 10 minutes COOKING TIME: 15 minutes

SERVES 4

300 g (11 oz) spaghetti or fettucine

grated rind and juice of 1 lemon

small bunch of fresh flat-leaf parsley

1 tablespoon capers

50 g (2 oz) small, sweet black olives

a pinch of crushed chilli flakes

4 tablespoons olive oil

1 large garlic clove

salt and freshly ground black pepper

Parmesan cheese, to serve

METHOD

1 Cook the pasta in a large pan of boiling, salted water according to packet instructions.

2 Meanwhile, put the rind and juice from the lemon into a large serving bowl. Roughly chop the parsley and capers and add to the bowl with the olives, chilli flakes and oil.

3 Crush in the garlic and season well.

4 Drain the pasta well and add to the bowl, tossing to mix. Shave or grate over some Parmesan and serve out at the table; remember to set out extra side bowls for spitting out the olive stones.

Paper potato pizza

A potato pizza sounds a little strange, but wait until you try it and you'll discover how delicious it is. Cut into thin wedges and serve warm or cold with Rocket and Roast Onion Salad (page 124) – although, I've never had it cold 'cos there's never any left.

PREPARATION: 20 minutes   COOKING TIME: 20 minutes

SERVES 4

150 g pack pizza-base mix

1 tablespoon olive oil

flour, for kneading

FOR THE TOPPING

250 g (9 oz) red-skinned or new potatoes

2 tablespoons olive oil, plus extra for drizzling

1 teaspoon fresh rosemary leaves

2 garlic cloves, crushed

sea salt and freshly ground black pepper

METHOD

1 Pre-heat the oven to 220°C/425°F/Gas 7. Place the pizza-base mix in a large bowl and stir in the olive oil and enough warm water (about 120 ml/ 4 fl oz) to make a soft dough. Knead vigorously on a lightly floured surface for about 5 minutes until smooth and elastic.

2 Roll the dough out to make a thin 30 cm (12 inch) circle. Transfer to a large baking sheet and set aside in a warm place for 5 minutes or so to rise.

3 Meanwhile, thinly slice the potatoes using a mandoline, food processor or the side of a box grater. Toss with the oil, rosemary, garlic and some salt and pepper.

4 Arrange the potato slices on the dough and bake for 10 minutes until risen and set. Slip off the baking sheet and continue to cook directly on the oven rack for a further 10 minutes until crisp and golden.

5 Drizzle over a little oil, scatter over some sea salt and a good grinding of black pepper. Cut into thin wedges and serve.

TRY THIS: Scatter over some thinly sliced pancetta, diced smoked bacon, Parmesan shavings or rocket leaves.

Paper potato pizza

Baked penne
with chorizo and Taleggio

Now this will tickle those taste buds. Baking pasta with cheese like this gives a really hearty, warming meal. Taleggio has a lovely flavour, but you could use Camembert or Port Salut instead. I've added chorizo, the spicy Spanish sausage that's flavoured with paprika: as it cooks, it releases its lovely juices into the dish. Absolutely scrumptious! Serve with a nice leafy salad drizzled with olive oil and splashed with your favourite balsamic vinegar.

PREPARATION: 15 minutes COOKING TIME: 15 minutes

SERVES 4

300 g (11 oz) penne

250 g carton mascarpone

2 teaspoons wholegrain mustard

4 salad onions, thickly sliced

250 g (9 oz) chorizo sausage, cut into chunks

200 g (7 oz) diced Taleggio cheese

salt and freshly ground black pepper

METHOD

1 Cook the pasta in a large pan of boiling, salted water according to the packet instructions.

2 Pre-heat the oven to 200°C/400°F/Gas 6. Drain the pasta well and return to the pan. Mix in the mascarpone and mustard, stirring until the mascarpone melts and coats the penne.

3 Stir in the salad onions, chorizo and cheese and season, then turn the mixture into an ovenproof dish. Bake for about 15–20 minutes until the top is crisp and golden brown.

Baked penne with chorizo and Taleggio

Buttered slam jackets

It really is hard to beat jacket potatoes when it comes to warming, nutritious and economical food. They make great accompaniments to a main meal, and with a tasty filling are satisfying by themselves. Begin by choosing a good main-crop potato, such as a King Edward or Desirée, as they have a desirable floury texture once cooked. If you like a soft skin on your potato, rub a little olive oil into the surface before baking; if you prefer a crunchier skin, leave the potato in the oven for 20 minutes or so longer. For extra-quick jackets, start in the microwave on high power for 8 minutes, then crisp up in a hot oven for 10–15 minutes.

You can bake new potatoes but you'll get a very different result as the flesh is firm and waxy. Rub baby new potatoes with oil and sprinkle with sea salt. Bake, then serve with, for example, my Lovely Tomato Chutney (page 142) or a cheesy fondue-style sauce for dipping into.

Whatever filling or topping I plan to serve my potatoes with, I always start with a knob of butter and a sprinkling of salt.

PREPARATION: 5 minutes COOKING TIME: 1½ hours

SERVES 1

1 large potato, weighing around 250 g (9 oz)

1 teaspoon olive oil

sea salt

small knob of butter

METHOD

1 Pre-heat the oven to 200°C/400°F/Gas 6. Scrub the potato and dry thoroughly. Prick in several places with a fork and rub in the olive oil; sprinkle lightly with sea salt. Bake for 1½ hours until the potato feels soft when gently squeezed.

2 Wrap the potato in a clean towel and slam down on to a board; alternatively, place the potato on a serving plate with a tea towel on top and hit it with your fist. Both these slamming methods work really well because the force breaks up the potato into fluffy grains and usually causes a natural split.

3 Drop the butter into the split and sprinkle in a little more salt. Eat immediately or serve with your choice of topping: Here are some of my favourites:
• soured cream and chives
• tuna and garlic mayo
• cream cheese and smoked salmon
• curried baked beans with mature Cheddar
• sautéed leeks, cream cheese and black pepper

Aubergine chilli jackets

My vegetarian friends simply love this recipe. It's quick, nutritious and extremely satisfying. For a touch of class, I like to serve it with a dollop of soured cream.

PREPARATION: 15 minutes COOKING TIME: 25 minutes

SERVES 4

2 tablespoons olive oil

1 onion, roughly chopped

2 garlic cloves, roughly chopped

1 red chilli, roughly chopped

2 large aubergines, cubed

2 teaspoons chopped fresh rosemary

150 ml (¼ pint) red wine

400 g can chopped plum tomatoes

400 g can cannellini beans, drained

sea salt and freshly ground black pepper

4 jacket potatoes (page 106)

METHOD

1 Heat the oil in a sauté pan and cook the onion, garlic and chilli for 2 minutes over a moderate heat. Add the aubergines and rosemary and continue to cook for a further 4–5 minutes until beginning to soften.

2 Pour in the wine and bring to the boil. Add the tomatoes and beans, season to taste, then cover and cook for 20–25 minutes or so, stirring from time to time.

3 Divide between hot, buttered jacket potatoes and serve straight away.

Fluffed, puffed cheese
and honey ham jackets

These jacket potatoes are a big hit in my house, especially with the children. The combination of honeyed ham and smoked mozzarella is absolutely delicious. Needless to say, ketchup is never requested…

PREPARATION: 15 minutes COOKING TIME: 20 minutes

SERVES 4

4 jacket potatoes (page 106)

knob of butter

1 tablespoon Dijon mustard

2 eggs, separated

100 g (4 oz) smoked mozzarella, diced

75 g (3 oz) honey-roast ham, roughly chopped

3 tablespoons snipped fresh chives

salt and freshly ground black pepper

green-leaf salad, to serve

METHOD

1 After taking the cooked potatoes out of the oven, lower the temperature to 180°C/350°F/Gas 4. Cut a 1 cm (½ inch) slice off the top of each potato and scoop out the flesh to leave a 5 mm (¼ inch) thick shell.

2 Mash the flesh with the butter, mustard and egg yolks. Stir in the cheese, ham, chives and some salt and pepper.

3 Whisk the egg whites until fairly stiff and fold into the potato mixture. Pile back into the shells and bake for 20 minutes until puffed and lightly browned. Serve hot with a crisp green-leaf salad.

Fluffed, puffed cheese and honey ham jackets

Jacqueline's potato skins
with guacamole

Crispy skins like these make really great party food, as well as an appetizing side dish. Serve them with a bowl of guacamole and also the soured cream dip from my Baconeese Cream Potato Wedges on page 112. The potato flesh can be saved and used to make my delicious Grate Hash Browns (page 117) for breakfast or brunch the next day. My sister Jacqueline likes to add a portion of the potato to her guacamole. It really works a treat, but you must mix it in well – ideally, using a food processor.

PREPARATION: 15 minutes   COOKING TIME: 20 minutes

SERVES 2

2 jacket potatoes (page 106)

2 tablespoons olive oil

coarse sea salt

FOR THE GUACAMOLE

1 large, ripe avocado, halved and stoned

1 garlic clove, crushed

1 red chilli, seeded and finely chopped

2 tablespoons chopped fresh coriander

juice of 1 lime

salt and freshly ground black pepper

METHOD

1 Bake the potatoes as described on page 102. Raise the oven temperature to 220°C/425°F/Gas 7. Halve the potatoes and scoop out the flesh to leave a 5 mm (¼ inch) thick shell. Cut each half into 3–4 strips, place in a bowl and toss with the oil.

2 Arrange the strips, skin-side down, on a sturdy baking sheet. Sprinkle with coarse sea salt and bake for 20 minutes or so until the strips are crisp and golden brown.

3 Next, make the guacamole: place the avocado flesh in a bowl and mash with a fork until fairly smooth. Stir in the garlic, chilli and coriander.

4 Add lime juice and salt and pepper to taste. Transfer to a bowl and serve with the crispy skins.

CHEF'S TIP: If you have any guacamole left over, squeeze fresh lemon or lime juice over it and cover with plastic wrap to help prevent discolouration.

Breaking bubble and Savoy squeak

Like Granny's Corned-Beef Hash and Fried Egg on page 89, this is also a quick, throw-it-together dish. It's great on its own with a steak or fried egg, but best of all, throw in some crispy bacon or diced spicy chorizo for a supper treat in front of the box.

PREPARATION: 15 minutes COOKING TIME: 20 minutes

SERVES 2

350 g (12 oz) floury potatoes, diced

half a small Savoy cabbage, shredded

2 tablespoons vegetable oil

1 small onion, chopped

2 garlic cloves, crushed

2 red chillies, thinly sliced

2 teaspoons Worcestershire or soy sauce

salt and freshly ground black pepper

METHOD

1 Cook the potatoes in a large pan of boiling, salted water for 8 minutes. Add the cabbage and cook for a further 3–4 minutes until tender.

2 Meanwhile, heat the oil in a large frying-pan and cook the onion, garlic and chillies for 5 minutes until golden.

3 Drain the potatoes and cabbage well and add to the frying-pan. Crush with a wooden spoon, then leave the mixture to cook over a medium heat for 2–3 minutes until a crust forms on the bottom.

4 Break up the mixture, stir in the Worcestershire or soy sauce and season, then leave to cook again until a crust forms on the bottom; break up again and cook for a third time. Spoon on to plates and serve.

CHEF'S TIP: Leave out the chilli if you're feeding this to kids.

Baconeese
cream potato wedges

The combination of bacon, cheese and potato is perfect. Add a chopped salad onion and soured cream and you're in heaven. I like to serve these wedges on the side with – and I know it sounds odd – the Classic Moules Marinière on page 69; they really taste fab together. Of course, you can serve them with all manner of other things, or on their own for a tasty snack.

PREPARATION: 15 minutes COOKING TIME: 40 minutes

SERVES 4

4 x 250 g (9 oz) baking potatoes

2 tablespoons olive oil

1 teaspoon paprika

½ teaspoon sea salt

75 g (3 oz) streaky bacon, chopped

100 g (4 oz) Gruyère or Cheddar, finely grated

4 salad onions, chopped

FOR THE DIP

300 ml (½ pint) soured cream

4 salad onions, finely chopped

1 teaspoon horseradish sauce

METHOD

1 Pre-heat the oven to 220°C/425°F/Gas 7. Cut each potato into 8 wedges and place in a bowl with the oil, paprika and salt. Toss well together, arrange on a sturdy baking sheet and cook for 20 minutes, turning occasionally. Scatter over the bacon and return to the oven for 10 minutes until the potatoes are cooked through and golden and the bacon is sizzling and crispy.

2 Scatter over the grated cheese and salad onions and return to the oven for a further 10 minutes until the cheese is melted and bubbly and the wedges are nicely browned.

3 Meanwhile, make the dip by stirring together the soured cream, salad onions and horseradish sauce. Spoon into a serving bowl, place the bowl into the centre of a large plate and arrange the cheesy wedges around the dip, scraping any cheese and bacon pieces on top of the wedges. Serve hot.

TRY THIS: If you have any left-over boiled or baked potatoes, cut them roughly into cubes and toss with the oil and paprika as before. Scatter with bacon and cook for 10 minutes, followed by the cheese for another 10 minutes. Hey presto, a scrumptious hash – great with a fried egg on top!

Baconeese cream potato wedges

Excellent egg and ginger fried rice

The secret to successful egg fried rice is to cook the eggs before you add the rice – it works a treat. With a touch more salad onion and ginger, this rice really titillates those taste buds.

PREPARATION: 5 minutes COOKING TIME: 10 minutes

SERVES 2

1 tablespoon vegetable oil

4 salad onions, thinly sliced

1 garlic clove, finely chopped

2 cm (¾ inch) piece fresh root ginger, grated or finely chopped

1 egg

175 g (6 oz) cooked long-grain rice

50 g (2 oz) frozen peas

1 tablespoon soy sauce

freshly ground black pepper

METHOD

1 Heat the oil in a wok and cook the salad onions, garlic and ginger for 2 minutes. Crack in the egg and scramble with a chopstick for a couple of minutes until just set.

2 Stir in the rice and peas and continue to cook for a further 3–4 minutes until piping hot. Season with soy sauce and a few twists of black pepper and serve.

CHEF'S TIP: If I don't have any left-over cooked rice to hand, I use frozen rice. It comes in free-flow bags and works brilliantly in stir-fries and other quick dishes. Buy it at your freezer store or supermarket.

Perfect golden, crispy chips

People often ask me how to make the perfect chips that are crunchy on the outside and fluffy in the centre. Well, here you have it and you don't even need an electric fryer. Remember to do the bread test for perfect results.

PREPARATION: 5 minutes COOKING TIME: 10 minutes

SERVES 1

1 large potato

vegetable oil, for frying

cubes of bread, to test oil temperature

salt

METHOD

1 Scrub the potato in clean, cold water and cut into fingers as thick or thin as you choose. Wash well to rinse off the excess starch and help prevent them sticking together during cooking. Dry thoroughly with kitchen paper.

2 Heat 5 cm (2 inches) vegetable oil in a small, deep frying-pan. Test the oil temperature with a cube of bread – it should take 60 seconds to turn brown. When the oil has reached the right temperature – do not let it get too hot – cook the chips for 5 minutes or until pale golden.

3 Remove with a slotted spoon and drain on kitchen paper. Raise the heat slightly and, when the oil is hot enough to brown a cube of bread in 30 seconds, return the chips to the pan for 1–2 minutes until crisp and golden. Drain on kitchen paper, sprinkle with salt, splash with malt vinegar and eat immediately.

Sesame prawn toasts

Once you've tried these prawn toasties, you'll be making them again and again – they're so easy to do. Great with my Hot and Sour Chicken and Mushroom Soup (page 50), they also make a fantastic, very attractive and quick snack. Now that's what I call impressive.

PREPARATION: 10 minutes COOKING TIME: 5 minutes

SERVES 4

175 g (6 oz) cooked peeled prawns

2 cm (¾ inch) piece fresh root ginger, grated

1 garlic clove, finely chopped

1 egg white

2 teaspoons cornflour

¼ teaspoon Chinese five-spice powder

¼ teaspoon salt

4 thin slices of bread, crusts removed

2 tablespoons sesame seeds

vegetable oil, for shallow-frying

METHOD

1 Place the prawns, ginger and garlic in a mini chopper or food processor and whizz until finely minced.

2 Whisk the egg white until frothy, then stir in the prawn mixture, cornflour, Chinese five-spice powder and salt until well blended.

3 Spread the mixture evenly on to the bread, then sprinkle over the sesame seeds, pressing them in firmly with the fingertips. Cut each slice into 4 squares, fingers or triangles.

4 Heat about 3–4 tablespoons of oil in a frying-pan; when hot, reduce the heat before adding the toasts. Cook prawn-side down for 2–3 minutes until golden, then turn and cook the other side – you might need a little more oil. Drain on kitchen paper and serve warm.

Grate hash browns

For a tasty treat, these hash browns are a perfect snack on their own. But I often make them for a weekend brunch served with my favourite sausages and cheesy baked beans.

PREPARATION: 5 minutes COOKING TIME: 25 minutes

SERVES 2

2 small, floury potatoes

salt and freshly ground black pepper

vegetable oil, for frying

METHOD

1 Cook the whole potatoes in a pan of boiling, salted water for 15 minutes until just tender. Drain and cool slightly.

2 Coarsely grate the potatoes into a bowl and season generously. Firmly shape the mixture into 4 oval patties by patting the mixture together with the palms of your hands.

3 Heat a little oil in a large frying-pan and cook the hash browns for 3–4 minutes on each side until crisp and golden. Drain on kitchen paper and serve hot.

TRY THIS: Add a nice touch of green with a few fresh chopped herbs – my favourite is thyme.

Garlic and parsley frittata

A frittata is simply an Italian omelette that you can add all sorts of ingredients to. It has a great taste with a lovely springy texture courtesy of the bread. A white slice will do, but you could be more adventurous. Serve with a watercress salad.

PREPARATION: 10 minutes COOKING TIME: 10 minutes

SERVES 1

2 tablespoons milk

2 eggs

1 tablespoon chopped fresh parsley

1 garlic clove, crushed

pinch of dried chilli flakes (optional)

1 slice white bread, torn into small pieces

sea salt and freshly ground black pepper

1 tablespoon olive oil

1 tablespoon freshly grated Parmesan

watercress salad, to serve

METHOD

1 Beat together the milk, eggs, parsley, garlic and chilli flakes, if using. Add the torn bread and some salt and pepper; set aside for 5 minutes so that the bread completely softens into the mixture.

2 Heat the oil in a 20 cm (8 inch) frying-pan and pour in the egg mixture. Cook for 3 minutes or so until golden and almost set.

3 Slide the frittata on to a plate, then turn the pan over on top of the plate and carefully flip over so you can cook the other side. Scatter over the Parmesan. Cook for a further couple of minutes until the underside is golden, the cheese has melted and the frittata is cooked through. Serve with a fresh, crisp watercress salad and a glass of your favourite Chianti.

Garlic and parsley frittata

Tabletop naan
with spicy fried onions

I've often eaten this in Indian restaurants, and it's always so yummy, with such a great taste and texture. I've put together a recipe for making it yourself and it's certainly worth the effort.

PREPARATION: 30 minutes COOKING TIME: 25 minutes

SERVES 2

450 g (1 lb) plain flour

pinch of salt

½ teaspoon baking powder

¼ teaspoon bicarbonate of soda

1 teaspoon caster sugar

1 egg

150 g carton natural yoghurt

4 tablespoons milk

2 tablespoons vegetable oil

25 g (1 oz) butter, melted

FOR THE SPICY ONIONS

2 tablespoons vegetable oil

2 onions, thinly sliced

2 teaspoons garam masala

½ teaspoon caster sugar

½ teaspoon table salt

METHOD

1 Pre-heat the oven to 220°C/425°F/Gas 7. Sift the flour, salt, baking powder and bicarbonate of soda into a bowl. Stir in the sugar.

2 In a separate bowl, whisk together the egg, yoghurt, milk and oil. Pour into the flour mixture and bring together to make a soft dough. Knead briefly, cover with oiled plastic wrap and set aside for 15 minutes.

3 For the spicy onions, heat the oil in a pan and cook the onions with the garam masala, sugar and salt for 15 minutes until golden brown.

4 Roll the dough out into a large rectangle. Using your fingers, press the dough into a swiss-roll tin. Scatter over the spicy onions, pressing them into the surface of the dough with the back of a spoon. Bake for 10 minutes until puffed and browned. Remove, brush with the melted butter and serve warm.

Green onion chapatis

I find chapatis really useful. They're easy to make and you can add all manner of extra flavourings – in this case salad onions. They're wonderful with curries, and the perfect accompaniment for many other dishes. You can buy chapati flour, basically a very fine flour, from an Indian grocer, but otherwise, use half ordinary wholemeal and half plain flour as I have done here. I stick to the authentic method by not adding any salt, but you can add a little if you prefer.

PREPARATION: 15 minutes COOKING TIME: 15 minutes

MAKES 12

150 g (5 oz) plain flour, plus extra for dusting

150 g (5 oz) fine wholemeal flour

4 salad onions, very finely chopped

METHOD

1 Sift the flours into a large bowl and stir in the salad onions. Gradually add 200 ml (7 fl oz) cold water to make a fairly firm dough. Knead vigorously for 5 minutes, then cover with a damp tea towel and set aside to rest.

2 Heat a heavy-based frying-pan or griddle, ideally cast-iron, but otherwise non-stick. Divide the dough into 12 balls, dust with flour and roll out into rough 15 cm (6 inch) rounds. Pass the rounds from hand to hand to shake off any excess flour.

3 Cook each chapati in the hot pan for a minute or so on each side until golden and a little puffed. Stack on a plate and keep covered until all the chapatis are cooked, remembering to wipe out the pan with kitchen paper between each chapati. Serve warm.

CHEF'S TIP: Left-over chapatis can be successfully re-heated in the microwave. Sprinkle a little water on each chapati and re-heat on high power for about 20 seconds or so.

Mozzamary garlic bread

Classic garlic bread with mozzarella cheese and rosemary makes a tasty accompaniment or side dish, but I find it particularly well suited to a bowl of steaming soup, such as the Roasted Tomato and Crème Fraîche Soup on page 46.

PREPARATION: 10 minutes COOKING TIME: 20 minutes

SERVES 4

150 g ball of mozzarella, drained

50 g (2 oz) butter, at room temperature

2 garlic cloves, crushed

2 teaspoons chopped fresh rosemary

¼ teaspoon salt

freshly ground black pepper

1 baguette

METHOD

1 Pre-heat the oven to 200°C/400°F/Gas 6. Roughly chop the mozzarella and place in a food processor with the butter, garlic, rosemary, salt and pepper. Whizz together to form a coarse paste.

2 Diagonally slice into the baguette at 2.5 cm (1 inch) intervals, taking care not to slice right through the base.

3 Spread the mozzarella mixture between the slices of bread, smearing any left over across the top.

4 Wrap the loaf in foil, making sure the ends are well sealed, but leaving the top open so that it can crust up in the oven. Bake for 20 minutes until the butter has melted and the cheese is bubbling; serve immediately.

CHEF'S TIP: If the baguette is too long to fit into your oven, just cut into 2 even-lengths and wrap individually.

Fern's creamy, crispy onion rings

Now here's a Fern favourite I've prepared many a time on *Ready Steady Cook,* as it's easy, goes with so many things and presents beautifully. If you have more time than I did – without Fern asking, 'What's in there?' – soak the onions in milk longer for really creamy, crispy onion rings.

PREPARATION: 5 minutes + soaking time COOKING TIME: 5 minutes

SERVES 2

1 Spanish onion

150 ml (¼ pint) milk

6 tablespoons seasoned flour

vegetable oil, for frying

METHOD

1 Slice the onion into 1 cm (½ inch) wide slices, then separate the rings. Place in a bowl with the milk and set aside for 5–30 minutes (depending on how much time you can spare – the longer the better).

2 Heat 5 cm (2 inches) of vegetable oil in a deep frying-pan.

3 Drain the onion rings, dust in the seasoned flour, then fry in batches for 2–3 minutes until crisp and golden. Drain on kitchen paper and eat hot.

Rocket
and roast onion salad

Roasted onions are absolutely delicious, but you don't see them that often. I like to serve them hot as a side vegetable, but they also make an extra-special salad when tossed with peppery rocket and salty Parmesan or Pecorino.

PREPARATION: 10 minutes COOKING TIME: 30 minutes

SERVES 4

12 button onions, halved

3 tablespoons olive oil

sea salt and coarsely ground black pepper

1 tablespoon balsamic vinegar

50 g (2 oz) Parmesan or Pecorino

100 g (4 oz) rocket leaves

METHOD

1 Pre-heat the oven to 190°C/375°F/Gas 5. Place the onions in a shallow roasting tin and drizzle over the oil. Season generously and roast for 25–30 minutes until the onions are softened and nicely browned.

2 Drizzle over the balsamic vinegar and allow the onions to cool to room temperature.

3 Using a swivel-style peeler, shave the cheese into wafer-thin slices.

4 Arrange the rocket, roast onions and cheese on 4 serving plates; drizzle round the pan juices and serve.

Rocket and roast onion salad

Pulao rice

Rice makes the perfect accompaniment to many Indian dishes, such as my tasty Lightning Lamb Dhansak (page 90). I've kept my pulao rice quite simple so that it doesn't mask the flavour of the curry you're serving with it.

PREPARATION: 20 minutes COOKING TIME: 25 minutes

SERVES 6

4 tablespoons vegetable oil

3 onions, thinly sliced

1 cinnamon stick

1 teaspoon cumin seeds

3 cardamom pods, cracked

3 star anise

500 g (1 lb 2 oz) basmati rice, rinsed

2 teaspoons salt

handful fresh coriander leaves

METHOD

1 Heat the oil in a large pan and cook half the onions over a fairly high heat for about 10 minutes until crisp and lightly browned. Drain on kitchen paper and set aside, leaving just a coating of oil still in the pan.

2 Add the remaining onions to the pan with the cinnamon, cumin, cardamom and star anise and cook gently for 5 minutes or so until the onions are golden.

3 Add the rice, cook for 1 minute, then add 1 litre (1¾ pints) of cold water and the salt. Bring to the boil, cover and cook over a low heat for 12 minutes until the grains are tender and the water has been absorbed.

4 Remove from the heat and leave to stand, covered, for 5 minutes. Transfer to a serving dish and scatter over the fried onions and coriander leaves; serve warm.

Warm sweet potato
and roast tomato cheese salad

A lovely combination of flavours that works surprisingly well and has instantly become a favourite among friends.

PREPARATION: 15 minutes COOKING TIME: 40 minutes

SERVES 4

500 g (1 lb 2 oz) sweet potatoes, cubed

1 garlic bulb, broken into cloves

3 tablespoons olive oil

1 teaspoon cumin seeds

8 fresh basil leaves, shredded

sea salt and freshly ground black pepper

4 small vines of cherry tomatoes, each with about 5 tomatoes

75 g (3 oz) strong blue cheese, e.g. Gorgonzola or Stilton

1 tablespoon red wine vinegar

METHOD

1 Pre-heat the oven to 200°C/400°F/Gas 6. Toss together the sweet potatoes, garlic, 1 tablespoon of the oil, the cumin seeds, basil and some salt and pepper.

2 Arrange on a baking sheet or shallow roasting tin and cook for 25 minutes. Add the tomato vines, trying to keep them intact – if there's not enough room in the tin, place the tomatoes on a separate baking sheet. Drizzle over a little more oil and cook for a further 15 minutes until the tomatoes are softened.

3 Lift off the tomatoes and set aside. Pile the sweet potatoes on to 4 serving plates and scatter over the crumbled blue cheese. Place a tomato vine on top of each and drizzle round a little more oil and a splash of red wine vinegar. Serve warm.

Spicy Spanish patatas bravas

Based on authentic *patatas bravas*, which translates as 'wild potatoes', this dish contains spices that certainly give a fiery flavour, while the cooking aroma gets the juices flowing early. Serve with a bowl of garlic mayonnaise or some of my Lovely Tomato Chutney (page 142).

PREPARATION: 10 minutes COOKING TIME: 40 minutes

SERVES 4

500 g (1 lb 2 oz) baby new potatoes

2 tablespoons olive oil

2 teaspoons paprika

2 teaspoons chilli powder

1 teaspoon ground cumin

1 teaspoon sea salt

1 tablespoon finely chopped fresh parsley

METHOD

1 Pre-heat the oven to 200°C/400°F/Gas 6. Place the potatoes in a strong plastic bag and bash with a rolling pin to crack them. Add the oil, paprika, chilli powder, cumin, sea salt and parsley to the bag, then shake well to mix.

2 Empty the potatoes on to a baking sheet and spread out into a single layer. Roast for 40 minutes, shaking the tray occasionally, until cooked through and nicely browned.

Minted
mushy chip-shop peas

OK, so you could just open a can – but home-made mushy peas really are terrific (and don't need to be that lurid green). I love to serve them with my Deep-fried Cod in Beer Batter (page 61) and Perfect Golden, Crispy Chips (page 115). Soaking the peas takes a little time, but after that this recipe is really quick, easy and so much cheaper than the canned variety.

PREPARATION: 2 hours COOKING TIME: 20 minutes

SERVES 6

250 g (9 oz) quick-soak dried peas

1 teaspoon sea salt

4 tablespoons malt vinegar

1 tablespoon mint sauce

sea salt and freshly ground black pepper

METHOD

1   Soak the peas for 2 hours or according to the packet instructions.

2   Drain the peas and place in a pan with 450 ml (¾ pint) of cold water. Bring to the boil and simmer for 20 minutes until the mixture is tender and thickened.

3   Stir in the salt, vinegar and mint sauce, and season to taste. Serve warm.

CHEF'S TIP: Left-over mushy peas keep very well for a few days, covered, in the fridge. Re-heat in the microwave.

Hail Caesar salad

The original dressing for this didn't contain anchovies as is commonly thought, so those of you who don't like them needn't miss out. Just sit back and enjoy this classic, which will be around for ever. Hail Caesar!

PREPARATION: 15 minutes

SERVES 4-6

1 cos lettuce

6–8 tinned anchovies, chopped

100 g (4 oz) Parmesan, grated

FOR THE DRESSING

1 large egg

1 garlic clove, roughly chopped

juice of 1 lime or ½ lemon

2 teaspoons English mustard powder

few shakes of Worcestershire sauce

150 ml (¼ pint) olive oil

sea salt and freshly ground black pepper

METHOD

1 Make the dressing: place the egg in a food processor with the garlic, lime or lemon juice, mustard powder and Worcestershire sauce. With the motor running, slowly pour in the oil to make a smooth sauce about the thickness of single cream. Season to taste and chill until ready to serve.

2 To make a classic Caesar salad, tear up the lettuce leaves and mix with the chopped anchovies and grated Parmesan. Drizzle with the dressing and scatter over a few Roasted Parmesan Croûtons (page 132).

TRY THIS: The dressing also tastes great drizzled over chicken or large grilled prawns.

Hail Caesar salad

Roasted Parmesan croûtons

These cheesy croûtons are really useful for tossing into bowls of soup and scattering over salads – they add flavour and that all-important crunch. I find that cooking them in the oven gives an even browning and means you can add less oil than when frying them.

PREPARATION: 5 minutes COOKING TIME: 10 minutes

SERVES 2

2 thick slices country-style bread

1 tablespoon olive oil

1 tablespoon finely grated Parmesan

1 garlic clove, crushed

salt and freshly ground black pepper

METHOD

1 Pre-heat the oven to 190°C/375°F/Gas 5. Slice the crusts off the bread and discard. Cut the bread into cubes and toss with the olive oil, Parmesan, garlic and salt and pepper. Scatter on to a baking sheet and cook in the oven for 10 minutes until crisp and golden.

2 Allow to cool a little, then serve.

TRY THIS: Ciabatta and flavoured focaccia, such as those made with olives or sun-dried tomato, make fantastic croûtons.

New millennium posh potato salad

I like to serve my new potato salad while it's still a little warm, but it's nearly as good after a day in the fridge. You can't beat a warm potato salad like this – it's totally comforting and, once on the table, is always the first salad to disappear, so make plenty.

PREPARATION: 15 minutes COOKING TIME: 10 minutes

SERVES 6

500 g (1 lb 2 oz) baby new potatoes, halved

75 g (3 oz) cubed pancetta or lardons

1 garlic clove, crushed

4 anchovies in oil, drained

4 tablespoons mayonnaise

4 salad onions, thinly sliced

salt and freshly ground black pepper

METHOD

1 Cook the potatoes in a pan of boiling, salted water for 10 minutes or so, until just tender.

2 Meanwhile, cook the pancetta in a non-stick frying-pan for 3–4 minutes until crisp and golden brown; drain on kitchen paper.

3 Drain the potatoes in a colander and leave to cool a while.

4 Make the dressing: mash together the garlic and anchovies then mix with the mayo. Toss with the warm potatoes, salad onions and crispy bacon, season with pepper and serve.

Citrus couscous and sultana salad

For a vegetarian treat, you simply can't beat this audacious salad with its wonderful colours, textures and flavour, which make it absolutely delicious.

PREPARATION: 20 minutes

SERVES 4

175 g (6 oz) couscous

300 ml (½ pint) hot vegetable stock

grated rind and juice of 1 lemon

2 small garlic cloves

200 g carton Greek yoghurt

a pinch of caster sugar

salt and freshly ground black pepper

3 tablespoons olive oil

1 red onion, finely chopped

400 g can chick peas, drained and rinsed

2 tablespoons roughly chopped fresh coriander, plus sprigs to garnish

50 g (2 oz) small sultanas

METHOD

1 Place the couscous in a large heatproof bowl and pour over the hot stock, then add the lemon rind and juice. Set aside for 10 minutes or so until the liquid has been absorbed.

2 Meanwhile, crush the garlic cloves into the yoghurt, add the sugar and season to taste; set aside.

3 Using a fork, lightly stir the couscous to separate the grains, then gently mix in the olive oil, onion, chick peas, coriander and sultanas. Add salt and pepper to taste. At this stage the salad can be chilled until ready to serve.

4 Divide the salad between 4 side bowls and spoon some of the garlic yoghurt on top of each. Lightly ripple it through the top of the salad, then garnish each bowl with a coriander sprig.

Citrus couscous and sultana salad

SAUCES & RELISHES

Maddie's mango chutney

This is a simple chutney with a lovely flavour that develops over time. It's worth the effort of making it yourself as it's so much nicer than commercially made varieties. Keep it in the fridge – I can't tell you how long it will store because it always gets eaten way too quickly in my house. Ask my daughter Maddie…

PREPARATION: 20 minutes COOKING TIME: 40 minutes

MAKES 900 ml (1½ pints)

4 garlic cloves, roughly chopped

2.5 cm (1 inch) piece root ginger, coarsely grated

1 red chilli, seeded and roughly chopped

½ teaspoon ground turmeric

1 teaspoon cayenne pepper

350 ml (12 fl oz) white wine vinegar

2 large green mangoes, cut into 2 cm (¾ inch) cubes

1 teaspoon salt

400 g (14 oz) golden caster sugar

4 tablespoons sultanas

1 star anise

METHOD

1 Place the garlic, ginger, chilli, turmeric, cayenne and a splash of the vinegar in a mini-chopper or food processor and blitz to a smooth paste.

2 Put the paste in a large pan with the remaining vinegar, the mangoes, salt, sugar, sultanas and star anise. Bring to the boil and simmer for 1 hour or so until the mixture has thickened – don't worry if it stills looks a little watery, as it will thicken further on cooling. Pour into a clean jar, seal and allow to cool. Now, where's that ham sandwich?

Easy mint chutney

If you like a bit on the side, this delicious relish goes with all manner of starters and curries. Try it with Sage and Onion Bhajis (page 12), Celtic Samosas (page 13) and Crispy Crunchy Sweetcorn Fritters (page 43). Any left-over chutney can be stirred into natural yoghurt and served with poppadoms and strips of toasted pitta. Or why not make it to go with that take-away curry you've just ordered?

PREPARATION: 5 minutes

SERVES 4

4 mild green chillies, seeded and roughly chopped

25 g (1 oz) fresh mint, chopped

15 g (½ oz) fresh coriander, chopped

2 teaspoons caster sugar

1 teaspoon garam masala

½ teaspoon table salt

juice of 1 lemon

METHOD

1 Place the chillies, mint and coriander in a mini food processor or liquidizer and whizz until very finely chopped. You might need to stop the food processor from time to time and give the mixture a stir.

2 Add the sugar, garam masala, salt, lemon juice and a tablespoon or two of water. Whizz again until smooth, then chill until ready to serve.

CHEF'S TIP: As always, when using fresh, raw herbs, try not to make this too far ahead of time as the colour will fade.

Ainsley's curry sauce to go

It doesn't matter whether you're from Yorkshire or Yarmouth, you can't beat the taste of curry sauce with chips. When I'm making chips at home (see page 115), it's too much trouble to go out just for the sauce, so this is my own version and I think it's just like the real thing – dead gorgeous!

PREPARATION: 10 minutes COOKING TIME: 15 minutes

SERVES 4

1 tablespoon vegetable oil

1 onion, finely chopped

1 red apple, roughly chopped

300 ml (½ pint) vegetable stock

1 tablespoon curry paste

1 tablespoon cornflour

2 tablespoons frozen peas

2 tablespoons fruity brown sauce

salt and freshly ground black pepper

METHOD

1 Heat the oil in a pan and cook the onion and apple for 3–4 minutes until softened and beginning to brown. Stir in the stock and curry paste and simmer together for 5 minutes.

2 Dissolve the cornflour in a little water and stir into the sauce with the peas and brown sauce. Bring to the boil and simmer for 2–3 minutes. Season to taste and serve warm (preferably over freshly fried chips).

TRY THIS: I think the fruity brown sauce is the secret to the success of this recipe, but if you don't have any, try it with regular brown sauce or a tablespoon of sandwich pickle.

Real tartare sauce

It's really easy (and a lot nicer) to make your own tartare sauce using shop-bought mayonnaise rather than forking out the premium price charged for a jar of it. Yes, you might have to go out and buy your capers, gherkins and a few other items, but once made, it will keep in the fridge for a day or two. Calamari, whitebait and fried fish of any kind all taste great with a spoonful on the side.

PREPARATION: 10 minutes

SERVES 8

200 g jar mayonnaise

1 shallot, very finely chopped

2 tablespoons pickled capers, well rinsed and roughly chopped

2 gherkins, roughly chopped

2 teaspoons horseradish sauce

1 teaspoon English mustard

3 tablespoons finely chopped fresh parsley

METHOD

Mix all the ingredients together. Cover and chill until ready to serve.

TRY THIS: Add a squeeze of fresh lemon juice for an extra kick, or a sprinkling of cayenne pepper for an extra, extra kick.

Lovely tomato chutney

This is a really versatile chutney. I love it in a nice cheesy toasted sandwich, on the side with a ploughman's lunch, or dolloped on top of my Wrap and Roll Hot Dogs (page 26). Ooh, lovely!

PREPARATION: 10 minutes COOKING TIME: 60 minutes

MAKES 850 g (1 lb 14 oz)

1 kg (2¼ lb) ripe tomatoes, roughly chopped

1 large onion, chopped

3 garlic cloves, finely chopped

150 ml (¼ pint) white wine vinegar

200 g (7 oz) light brown sugar

1 teaspoon salt

½ teaspoon dried chilli flakes

4 cardamom pods, cracked

¼ teaspoon ground cinnamon

METHOD

1 Place all the ingredients in a large pan. Bring to the boil and simmer for 60 minutes, stirring fairly frequently until thickened and pulpy.

2 Remove from the heat and stir occasionally until cool, then pour into a clean jar, seal and allow to cool completely.

Char-grilled vegetables and hummus ciabatta *with* Lovely tomato chutney

Banana raita

This gorgeous raita is so refreshing and is the perfect accompaniment to curry and spicy dishes. My wife likes to make it just before the take-away arrives.

PREPARATION: 5 minutes

SERVES 2

1 ripe banana

1 garlic clove, crushed

150 g carton natural yoghurt

juice of ½ lemon

¼ teaspoon salt

METHOD

Mash the banana well with a fork and mix with the garlic and yoghurt. Add lemon juice and salt to taste. Serve immediately.

Red onion relish

This relish is particularly nice scattered on top of a plain salad, or equally delicious in a cheesy tomato sandwich. To toast the cumin seeds, use a dry frying-pan set over a medium heat and cook them for 2–3 minutes, stirring all the time.

PREPARATION: 15 minutes

SERVES 4

2 red onions, thinly sliced

½ teaspoon table salt

½ teaspoon cumin seeds, toasted

2 tablespoons red wine vinegar

1 red chilli, seeded and finely chopped

1 teaspoon caster sugar

2 tablespoons chopped coriander

METHOD

1 Place the red onions in a bowl. Sprinkle over the salt and set aside for 10 minutes.

2 Pat the onions dry and mix with the remaining ingredients. Chill until ready to serve.

Soy dipping sauces

I've got two favourite ways of making this – the first one is a little more fiery than the other. As you get used to the flavours, you can adjust the quantities to suit your taste.

Floating chilli soy dipping sauce

For this you need to use an authentic chilli oil from an oriental grocer. This contains shrimp paste, so it has more depth than a Mediterranean-style chilli oil, which is normally just olive oil and chillies.

PREPARATION: 2 minutes

SERVES 2

4 tablespoons soy sauce

1 teaspoon rice vinegar or white wine vinegar

¼ teaspoon chilli oil

pinch of chilli flakes (optional)

METHOD

Mix all the ingredients together well and serve. The chilli flakes are optional, but look and taste wonderful.

Sweet soy sesame dipping sauce

Preparation: 5 minutes

SERVES 4

3 tablespoons soy sauce

2 tablespoons sake or dry sherry

1 tablespoon brown sugar

½ teaspoon sesame seeds

METHOD

Mix all the ingredients together, stirring until the sugar dissolves.

Sweet chilli sauce

I usually make up big batches of this and keep it in the fridge because it's so handy for adding to other dishes for a little extra heat and sweetness – and, of course, it's a great accompaniment to all kinds of dishes, such as Celtic Samosas (page 13), Crispy Cache Calamari (page 73) and Pacific Prawn Fu-yung (page 60).

PREPARATION: 5 minutes COOKING TIME: 5 minutes

SERVES 4

1 tablespoon sunflower oil

1 onion, chopped

2 garlic cloves, finely chopped

2 red chillies, finely chopped

juice of 1 orange

1 tablespoon clear honey

1 tablespoon malt vinegar

2 tablespoons tomato ketchup

METHOD

1 Heat the oil in a small pan and cook the onion for 2–3 minutes over a medium heat.

2 Add the garlic and chillies and continue to cook for a further 2 minutes, stirring occasionally, until softened.

3 Stir in the orange juice, honey, vinegar and tomato ketchup and heat through gently until just beginning to bubble. Remove from the heat, cool slightly and serve.

Mama Tahsia's tzatziki

Tzatziki is a Greek classic, so refreshing on the palate, and perfect for jazzing up kebabs, salads and my recipe for Dimitri's Festive Feta Triangles (page 40).

PREPARATION: 10 minutes

SERVES 4

½ cucumber

200 g carton Greek yoghurt

4 tablespoons chopped fresh mint

2 garlic cloves, crushed

pinch of dried oregano

pinch of caster sugar

juice of 1 lime

salt and freshly ground black pepper

METHOD

Grate the cucumber into a sieve set over a bowl, or finely dice. Try to avoid using the central seeded core as it's very watery. Squeeze out any excess water by presssing the cucumber down into the sieve and transfer to a bowl. Add the yoghurt, mint, garlic, oregano, caster sugar and lime juice. Season to taste and chill until ready to use. Garnish with a sprig of mint and serve with olives and triangles of pitta bread.

Portuguese custard tarts

This is one of the best ways I know to finish off a sunny lunch – brilliant with an espresso.

PREPARATION: 20 minutes COOKING TIME: 20 minutes

MAKES 16

75 g (3 oz) golden caster sugar

2 tablespoons cornflour

450 ml (¾ pint) milk

2 egg yolks

1 teaspoon vanilla extract

375 g pack ready-rolled puff pastry

plain flour for rolling

METHOD

1 Place the sugar in a pan with 5 tablespoons of water and gently bring to the boil, stirring until the sugar dissolves.

2 Dissolve the cornflour in a little of the milk. Whisk the remaining milk, the egg yolks, vanilla extract and cornflour mixture into the sugar syrup. Gently bring to the boil, stirring continuously, until smooth and thickened. Cover the custard and allow to cool.

3 Open out the sheet of pastry and roll out a little more to a thickness of 3 mm (⅛ inch). Stamp out the pastry into 10 cm (4 inch) circles and use them to line a small bun tin (the pastry might come further up the sides of each tin than usual, but it will shrink as it cooks). Refrigerate until the custard is cool.

4 Preheat the oven to 200°C/400°F/Gas 6. Spoon the cooled custard into the tart cases and bake for 20 minutes until the tarts are golden brown. Serve warm or at room temperature.

Portuguese custard tarts

Spider doughnuts

Real doughnuts take ages to prepare because they're made from a yeasted dough that needs to rise. My version uses a thick batter, which cooks to make puffy, spidery-shaped rounds. Serve them with a dip made from lightly whipped double cream and lemon curd, or cut them in half and sandwich back together with strawberry jam.

PREPARATION: 15 minutes COOKING TIME: 15 minutes

SERVES 6

300 g (11 oz) plain flour, plus extra for rolling

1 teaspoon baking powder

¼ teaspoon table salt

2 tablespoons golden caster sugar

50 g (2 oz) butter, melted

200 ml (7 fl oz) milk

4 eggs, beaten

vegetable oil, for deep-frying

icing or golden caster sugar, for dusting

METHOD

1 Sift the flour, baking powder and salt into a large bowl. Stir in the sugar and make a well in the centre.

2 Stir in the butter, milk, eggs and 100 ml (3½ fl oz) water to make a smooth, thick batter.

3 Heat the oil in the pan and drop in small spoonfuls of the mixture; cook for 5 minutes until brown and cooked through. Drain on kitchen paper, then dust liberally with sugar and serve.

CHEF'S TIP: Try to make sure that the batter goes into the pan as a dollop rather than letting it trail off the spoon in a stream – this would give you long, snaky fritters instead of round spiders.

Lemon vanilla crêpes

You simply cannot beat a French-style crêpe with a sprinkling of sugar (vanilla sugar, in an ideal world) and a squeeze of fresh lemon juice.

PREPARATION: 15 minutes COOKING TIME: 15 minutes

SERVES 4 (makes about 8)

50 g (2 oz) plain flour

50 g (2 oz) caster sugar

2 eggs

300 ml (½ pint) milk

50 g (2 oz) butter, melted

vegetable oil, for shallow-frying

vanilla sugar or golden caster sugar

2 juicy lemons, cut into quarters

METHOD

1 Place the flour and sugar in a bowl. Crack in the eggs and gradually beat in the milk and butter to make a smooth, thin batter.

2 Heat about ½ teaspoon of oil in a crêpe pan or small frying-pan. Swirl in a thin coating of batter and cook until golden, flip over and cook the other side. Fold each pancake into halves or quarters and serve immediately with a sprinkling of sugar and splash of lemon juice.

FILL 'EM UP

If you feel like going the whole way, here's a couple of pancake fillers for you to try.

Mix together a 250 g carton of mascarpone with one tablespoon of sifted icing sugar (and maybe a splash of orange or coffee liqueur). Ripple through three tablespoons of ready-made chocolate sauce and spoon into warm pancakes before folding.

Place 250 g frozen summer berries in a bowl and sprinkle over 2 tablespoons of icing sugar. Allow to thaw for a few hours, then ripple in a 200 g carton of crème fraîche.

Iced caffe latte cups

I've taken my favourite milky coffee drink and turned it into a really simple but very stylish ice-cream dessert. Make this well ahead of time, but remember to place the cups in the fridge for 1 hour or so before serving so that the caffe latte can soften and you won't be in danger of bending your spoons.

PREPARATION: 5 minutes + freezing time

SERVES 6

4 tablespoons golden caster sugar

100 ml (3½ fl oz) freshly made espresso coffee

420 ml can evaporated milk

300 ml (½ pint) single cream

handful roasted coffee beans

cantuccini or chocolate finger biscuits, to serve

METHOD

1 Stir the sugar into the coffee until dissolved. Mix in the evaporated milk and single cream.

2 Pour into six coffee cups and scatter four or five coffee beans on top of each. Freeze for several hours until frozen solid. About an hour before serving, transfer to the fridge, then serve with a biscuit or two on the side.

Simple saffron kulfi

Kulfi is a scrumptious Indian ice-cream that is often flavoured with fruit, such as mango, or nuts, such as pistachios. I've kept this very simple by just using saffron but, for a touch of luxury, I've topped each serving with a sliver of edible gold or silver leaf, which you can buy in cake shops or from art and craft shops. You need to stir the milk frequently so that it doesn't burn on the bottom of the pan.

PREPARATION: 5 minutes + freezing time   COOKING TIME: 5 minutes

SERVES 6

600 ml (1 pint) milk

2 large pinches of saffron

420 ml can evaporated milk

6 tablespoons caster sugar

METHOD

1 Place all the ingredients in a pan and heat gently, stirring until the sugar dissolves. Remove from the heat and allow to cool. Pour into individual moulds and freeze for at least 2 hours until solid.

2 Turn the kulfi out on to serving plates and top each with a sliver of gold or silver leaf; serve immediately.

TRY THIS: You can buy special conical-shaped moulds from Asian stores to freeze your desserts in – they're quite cheap. Alternatively, save a few empty yoghurt cartons, wash thoroughly and keep to use as your kulfi moulds.

Dad's
chocolate-chip coconut cookies

Warm cookies straight from the oven are a treat few can resist – ask my dad. However, if my children have been really, really good, I sandwich pairs of cookies together when they've slightly cooled with vanilla or lemon curd ice-cream.

PREPARATION: 15 minutes COOKING TIME: 15 minutes

MAKES 16

175 g (6 oz) butter, room temperature

175 g (6 oz) caster sugar

½ teaspoon vanilla extract

100 g (4 oz) plain flour

100 g (4 oz) self-raising flour

50 g (2 oz) desiccated coconut

150 g (5 oz) dark chocolate, roughly chopped

METHOD

1 Pre-heat the oven to 190°C/375°F/Gas 5. Using electric beaters, whisk together the butter, sugar and vanilla until pale and fluffy.

2 Sift in the flours, then fold in the coconut and chocolate.

3 Shape the mixture into balls, then roughly flatten out on 2 baking sheets with the palm of your hand, leaving room for them to spread slightly.

4 Bake for 15 minutes until lightly browned. Allow the cookies to cool for a few minutes, then eat while still warm. Alternatively, transfer to a wire rack and leave to cool completely. Store in an airtight jar until needed. Now, where's that ice-cream?

Ribbled raspberry
and white chocolate muffins

I've baked these muffins in parchment paper because it reminds me of breakfasting in continental cafés. Serve with a shot of espresso or a long milky coffee for a luxurious start to the day.

PREPARATION: 20 minutes COOKING TIME: 30 minutes

MAKES 8

300 g (11 oz) plain flour

2 teaspoons baking powder

150 g (5 oz) golden caster sugar

1 egg

1 teaspoon vanilla extract

225 ml (7½ fl oz) milk

50 g (2 oz) butter, melted

100 g (4 oz) fresh raspberries

75 g (3 oz) chopped white chocolate

METHOD

1 Pre-heat the oven to 200°C/400°F/Gas 6. Cut parchment or greaseproof paper into 8 x 15 cm (6 inch) circles and push, creasing the paper to fit, into a muffin tin.

2 Sift the flour and baking powder into a large bowl and stir in the sugar. Crack the egg into a separate bowl and whisk in the vanilla extract, milk and melted butter.

3 Stir the liquid into the dry ingredients with the raspberries and chocolate, taking care not to over-mix. Spoon the mixture into the parchment cases and bake for 30 minutes or so until well risen and just firm.

TRY THIS: Try making these muffins with other fruit, such as blueberries or diced strawberries.

Ribbled raspberry and white chocolate muffins

American dream pancakes

These lovely little pancakes make a great dessert or breakfast. Try adding some fresh fruit, such as blueberries or raspberries, to the batter, or stack them high and drizzle with runny honey or maple syrup and a dollop of clotted cream or crème fraîche. Oh, one could go on and on…

PREPARATION: 5 minutes COOKING TIME: 10–15 minutes

SERVES 4

2 eggs

5 tablespoons milk

150 g (5 oz) self-raising flour

2 tablespoons caster sugar

½ teaspoon salt

1 tablespoon vegetable oil, for frying

crème fraîche and ground cinnamon, to serve

METHOD

1 Whisk together the eggs and milk. Place the flour, sugar and salt in a large bowl, make a well in the centre, pour in the liquid and beat with a hand whisk until smooth.

2 Heat a little oil in a large non-stick frying-pan. Gently drop large spoonfuls of the pancake mixture into the hot pan and cook for 2 minutes until crisp and golden. Carefully turn and cook for 1 minute until golden.

3 Transfer the pancakes to serving plates, dust with a little cinnamon and top with a dollop of crème fraîche. Serve warm.

Sophisticated
strawberry sundae

They may be old-fashioned, but sundaes are such a decadent treat that it's time we saw more of them back in our parks and cafés. Here's the classic sundae, guaranteed to get you oooh-ing and aaah-ing. I've made it a touch more sophisticated by adding orange liqueur to the whipped cream, and it's marvellous.

PREPARATION: 10 minutes COOKING TIME: 5 minutes

SERVES 4

150 ml carton double cream

1 tablespoon icing sugar

2 tablespoons orange liqueur, such as Grand Marnier or Cointreau

8 scoops vanilla ice-cream

FOR THE STRAWBERRY SYRUP

500 g (1 lb 2 oz) fresh strawberries

juice of ½ lime

2 tablespoons caster sugar

1 teaspoon arrowroot

METHOD

1 Begin by making the syrup: save 8 of the best strawberries, then halve the remainder and place in a small pan with the lime juice and sugar. Cook for a few minutes until softened and pulpy.

2 Push through a fine sieve and return to the pan. Dissolve the arrowroot in a little water and stir the paste into the strawberry mixture. Gently bring to the boil, stirring, until slightly thickened, then remove from the heat and allow to cool.

3 Whisk together the double cream, icing sugar and liqueur until it forms soft peaks.

4 Cut the reserved strawberries into halves or quarters. Place 2 scoops of ice-cream in 4 sundae glasses and swirl over the cream, scattering in the strawberries as you go. Drizzle over the cooled syrup and serve for a classic, old-fashioned treat.

Banana splits
with warm choco-fudge sauce

Remember eating these at your local café? They work best if you've got glass banana-split dishes to serve them in. If you have only upright sundae glasses, cut the bananas into four and push them into the ice-cream.

PREPARATION: 10 minutes COOKING TIME: 5 minutes

SERVES 4

FOR THE FUDGE SAUCE

150 g (5 oz) dark chocolate

40 g (1½ oz) butter

150 ml carton double cream

100 g (4 oz) dark brown sugar

2 tablespoons golden syrup

FOR THE BANANA SPLITS

4 ripe bananas

12 scoops of ice-cream

150 ml carton double cream, softly whipped

12 glacé cherries

50 g (2 oz) chopped mixed nuts, toasted

8 fan-shaped wafers

METHOD

1 Begin by making the fudge sauce: break the chocolate into a pan and add the butter, cream, sugar and syrup. Heat gently, stirring, until the ingredients are melted and well blended; remove from the heat, but do not allow to cool completely.

2 Cut each banana in half lengthways and place in the banana-split dishes, pushing the halves apart. Place 2 scoops of ice-cream between 2 pieces of banana.

3 Spoon over the cream, then scatter over the cherries. Drizzle over the warm sauce, scatter over the nuts, then push in the wafers and serve immediately.

TRY THIS: Traditionally, each split would be topped with one scoop of chocolate ice-cream, one of vanilla and one of strawberry – like me, though, you might find it easier to choose just one or two flavours.

Banana splits with warm choco-fudge sauce

Angela's ribbons

My friend Angela gave this recipe to me – her Italian mother used to make it for her as a child. The ribbons are all different and look really attractive. Serve them warm with a fruit compote and cream as a dessert, or warm with hot chocolate for breakfast or before bed.

PREPARATION: 20 minutes + resting time COOKING TIME: 5 minutes

MAKES 18-20

250 g (9 oz) plain flour, plus extra for rolling

25 g (1 oz) golden caster sugar

grated rind and juice of 1 small orange

1 egg

1 egg yolk

25 g (1 oz) butter, melted

vegetable oil, for deep-frying

golden caster sugar or icing sugar, to dust

METHOD

1 Place the flour, sugar, orange rind and juice, egg, egg yolk and butter in a food processor and pulse to make a smooth dough. Roll into a ball, cover with plastic wrap and chill for an hour or so.

2 Heat 10 cm (4 inches) of vegetable oil in a wok or deep frying-pan.

3 Roll out the dough on a floured surface to a thickness of 5 mm (¼ inch). Cut into ribbons about 2 cm (¾ inch) wide and 15 cm (6 inches) long.

4 Deep-fry for a minute or two until crisp and golden. Remove with a slotted spoon and drain on kitchen paper. Dust with sugar and serve warm.

TRY THIS: Tie the ribbons in knots, or cut a slot in one end of a ribbon and thread the other end through to make a loop; then fry as normal.

Lychee, lime and cream frost

You can make this recipe with all sorts of fruit; you could even use a bag of frozen mixed summer fruits. For me, lychees are so refreshing, and the perfect way to end a Thai, Chinese or spicy meal.

PREPARATION: 5 minutes + 2 hours minimum freezing time

SERVES 4

400 g can lychees in syrup, drained

1 fresh or dried (kaffir) lime leaf, finely chopped, or grated rind of 1 lime

200 ml/7 fl oz double cream

METHOD

1 Line a plastic tray with greaseproof paper and scatter on the lychees, making sure they're not touching.

2 Freeze for at least a couple of hours until solid.

3 Place the frozen lychees in a food processor with the lime leaf. Turn on the motor and slowly pour in the double cream. As the cream hits the frozen lychees it will semi-freeze into a thickened, frosty mixture.

4 Divide between chilled glasses or bowls and serve.

Clare's heaven lemon cake

I love a slice of cake with a cup of tea, and this is a really simple one with a deliciously tart lemon flavour. It slices like a dream too. Clare, my wife, came up with the recipe.

PREPARATION: 15 minutes COOKING TIME: 30 minutes

SERVES 8

120 g (4½ oz) butter, at room temperature

175 g (6 oz) caster sugar

1½ tablespoons grated lemon rind (about 2 lemons)

2 eggs, beaten, at room temperature

120 ml (4 fl oz) soured cream

120 ml (4 fl oz) lemon juice (about 2 lemons)

350 g (12 oz) self-raising flour

METHOD

1 Pre-heat the oven to 180°C/350°F/Gas 4. Beat together the butter, sugar and lemon rind, using an electric whisk, until smooth and light. Beat in the eggs, soured cream and lemon juice.

2 Sift over the flour and carefully fold in with a metal spoon. Spoon into a greased and lined 20 cm (8 inch) cake tin and bake for 40 minutes until firm and springy to the touch. Allow to cool slightly before transferring to a wire rack.

3 Slice and serve warm with cream as a dessert, or cool completely and serve with a nice cup of tea.

TRY THIS: Make this scrumptious cake a little more child-friendly by topping it with a simple frosting: sweeten 200 g (7 oz) soft cheese with 2 tablespoons of sifted icing sugar, adding a little milk if the mixture is too stiff.

Clare's heaven lemon cake

Sweet 'n' easy mango lassi

Lassi is a refreshing yoghurt-based drink that's often combined with fruit. Mango is the classic fruit used for it (use tinned if you can't get hold of fresh), but this recipe also works very well if you substitute a large ripe banana. Whatever the fruit, it's the ideal accompaniment to hot or spicy dishes, as the yoghurt cools down the mouth far more efficiently than water.

PREPARATION: 5 minutes

SERVES 2

250 ml (8 fl oz) natural yoghurt

150 g (5 oz) chopped mango flesh

2 tablespoons caster sugar

METHOD

Blitz all the ingredients together in a blender or food processor. Pour into 2 ice-filled glasses and serve.

Fun fresh 'n' healthy juices

Juice bars are springing up all over the place – in fact, juice is the new coffee. If you've invested in an electric juicer, here's a couple of great-tasting, vitamin-packed, healthy drinks for you.

Stripy grape juice

1. Juice the fruit in the order given for a stripy ripple fruit juice.

2. Pass 2 green apples and about 25 white grapes through a juicer and pour into a glass. Now juice about 25 red grapes and pour into the same glass. Drink straight away.

Vegetable patch

Juice 1 ripe tomato, 2 large carrots and a celery stalk. Pour into an ice-filled glass, then add a squeeze of fresh lime juice; stir with a celery stick and serve.

Fresh cherryade

This is nothing like that over-sweet stuff you used to drink bottles of as a kid – no, this is a fragrant drink that's really refreshing and fantastic for picnics and barbecues. Just you watch it disappear.

PREPARATION: 10 minutes + cooling time COOKING TIME: 10 minutes

SERVES 4

400 g (14 oz) fresh cherries, plus extra for garnish

50 g (2 oz) caster sugar

1 sprig fresh tarragon

juice of 2 limes

600 ml (1 pint) soda water

ice and lime twists, to serve

METHOD

1 Place the cherries, sugar and tarragon in a small pan with 450 ml ($\frac{3}{4}$ pint) of water. Gently bring to the boil, stirring until the sugar dissolves, then simmer for 10 minutes until the cherries are very soft.

2 Remove from the heat, then pass through a sieve to remove the stones and tarragon and purée the cherries. Stir in the lime juice, then chill until ready to serve.

3 Transfer to a jug and top up with soda water. Pour into ice-filled glasses and serve garnished with lime twists and cherries.

Supercallifabulistic soda floats

Here's an old-fashioned Mary Poppins favourite. You can combine the flavours as you wish, but if you're using a fancy ice-cream, just serve it with plain soda water, and if you have a fancy fizzy drink, such as cola, serve it with plain vanilla ice-cream. Of course, you can always throw caution to the wind and try a whole host of wild combinations, but here are a few tried-and-tasted floats to be getting on with. In each case, place the ice-cream in a tall glass, pour over the fizz and serve immediately with straws for sipping. Don't forget the long spoons so you can reach the fizzy ice-cream at the bottom of the glass.

EACH FLOAT SERVES 1

Cola float

1 scoop vanilla ice-cream

250 ml (8 fl oz) cola

Orange soda

1 scoop vanilla ice-cream

250 ml (8 fl oz) orangeade

Chocolate soda

1 scoop chocolate/chocolate chip ice-cream

250 ml (8 fl oz) lemonade

Red berry float

1 scoop raspberry/strawberry ice-cream

250 ml (8 fl oz) limeade

Lemonade and vanilla ice-cream float

Watermelon smoothie

Pretty similar in fact to a lassi (page 170), smoothies have become increasingly popular as a healthy drink. I've tried many smoothies in my time and this is most definitely my favourite. Like other juice-based drinks, this is really smashing first thing in the morning. An average small watermelon weighs about 3 kg (7 lb), but you don't need to worry too much about the actual weight: just use more or less yoghurt to suit your fancy.

SERVES 2

½ small watermelon, about 1.5 kg (3¼ lb), peeled, seeded and cubed

150 g carton natural yoghurt

METHOD

1 Pass the watermelon through a juicer.

2 Place 8 ice cubes in a glass jug and mix with the yoghurt; pour in the watermelon juice, mixing well. Pour into glasses and drink immediately.

CHEF'S TIP: I use a juicer but you can whizz the whole thing up in a liquidizer if you don't have one.

Fresh cherryade *and* Watermelon smoothie

Cardamom-scented
hot chocolate and cream

There are lots of ways to make hot chocolate using cocoa powder or drinking chocolate, but the best flavour comes from melting real milk chocolate into warm milk. If I'm feeling really extravagant, I top each mug with a scoopful of vanilla ice-cream or a few marshmallows, followed by the grated chocolate. Total indulgence and a wonderful taste. Go on, get cardamom scented.

PREPARATION: 5 minutes COOKING TIME: 5 minutes

SERVES 4

1 litre (1¾ pints) milk

½ teaspoon ground cinnamon

4 cardamom pods, cracked

350 g (12 oz) milk chocolate

100 g (4 oz) extra thick cream

2 tablespoons finely grated dark chocolate, to decorate

METHOD

1 Place the milk in a large pan with the cinnamon and cardamom and heat gently. Break the chocolate into the pan and gently bring to the boil, stirring occasionally, until melted.

2 Scoop out the cardamom pods and discard. Pour the hot chocolate into four mugs and top each with a spoonful of extra thick cream; sprinkle over some grated chocolate and serve.

Cardamom-scented hot chocolate and cream *with* Dad's chocolate-chip coconut cookies

AINSLEY
HARRIOTT'S
GOURMET EXPRESS 2

Toasted halloumi cheese and chorizo skewers

Halloumi is a great cheese for grilling because it holds its shape when warmed and has a wonderful texture. It's now readily available from larger supermarkets, sometimes packed in water for freshness – make sure you drain it thoroughly and rinse it before use. To enjoy these delicious skewers at their best, make sure you eat them hot as they become quite chewy when cold.

PREPARATION: 20 minutes COOKING TIME: 10 minutes

SERVES 4

1 loaf flavoured focaccia (see Chef's Tip below)

70 g pack thin-cut chorizo

10 fresh basil leaves

250 g (9 oz) halloumi

2 tablespoons chilli oil

1 lemon, cut into wedges, to serve

METHOD

1   Halve the focaccia horizontally then arrange the chorizo slices, overlapping, across the base of the sandwich. Place the basil leaves on the chorizo then sandwich the bread back together. Using a serrated knife cut the sandwich into about 40 2.5 cm (1 inch) squares.

2   Cut the halloumi in half lengthways to make 2 long blocks roughly 2.5 cm (1 inch) thick. Now slice each block thinly to give a total of 32 square slices of cheese. Thread the halloumi and sandwich squares alternately on to 8 bamboo skewers, starting and ending each stick with a sandwich. Brush lightly with the chilli oil.

3   Heat a ridged griddle pan or heavy, non-stick frying-pan and cook the skewers for 2–3 minutes on each side until hot and golden brown. Serve garnished with lemon wedges.

CHEF'S TIP: A rectangular cheesy loaf measuring 13 x 20 cm (5 x 8 inches) is the perfect size for this recipe. If you have a round or oval loaf it doesn't matter – if some of the edges of the sandwiches are rounded or some squares are smaller than others, it all adds to the charm of the skewers. And if the cheese breaks or is uneven, thread it on – it'll still look great. Enjoy!

Toasted halloumi cheese and chorizo skewers

Black and blue Cajun-chicken sandwich

An American classic made in heaven.

PREPARATION: 10 minutes COOKING TIME: 10 minutes

SERVES 2

1 large skinless, boneless chicken breast, about 150 g (5 oz)

1 tablespoon plain flour

1 teaspoon cayenne

1 teaspoon ground mixed spice

½ teaspoon dried oregano

1–2 tablespoons vegetable oil for shallow-frying

4 thick slices crusty bread

2 tablespoons mayonnaise

¼ cucumber

salt and freshly ground black pepper

75 g (3 oz) blue cheese such as Gorgonzola or Stilton

METHOD

1 Cut the chicken breast in half horizontally. Place between two sheets of cling film and flatten with a rolling pin until 1 cm (½ inch) thick. Mix together the flour, cayenne, mixed spice, oregano, salt and pepper. Dust the chicken in the seasoned flour, shaking off any excess.

2 Heat the oil in a large frying-pan and cook the chicken for 5 minutes on each side until well browned and a little charred around the edges.

3 Meanwhile, toast the bread and spread two of the slices with mayonnaise. Thinly slice the cucumber and arrange over the mayonnaise. Place a piece of chicken on each, crumble over the blue cheese and top with the remaining slices of toast. Cut in half and serve warm.

CHEF'S TIP: You can make this dish more of a meal by serving the sandwich open with a rocket salad on the side.

Pancetta hash browns

Hash browns are an irresistible addition to any cooked breakfast. These crispy bacon wedges make an excellent snack in their own right and, when topped with a fried egg, a tasty brekkie treat.

PREPARATION: 20 minutes COOKING TIME: 15 minutes

SERVES 4

4 small floury potatoes, about 100 g (4 oz) each

75 g (3 oz) thin-sliced pancetta, roughly chopped

2 salad onions, thinly sliced

salt and freshly ground black pepper

METHOD

1 Cook the potatoes whole in a pan of boiling water for 15 minutes until just tender – don't worry if they're a little hard in the centre.

2 Heat a large, non-stick frying-pan and cook the pancetta for 2–3 minutes until golden. Remove with a slotted spoon and drain on kitchen paper.

3 Coarsely grate the potatoes, including the skin, into a large bowl, then stir in the pancetta, salad onions and some salt and pepper.

4 Return the mixture to the frying-pan and cook for 8 minutes until golden. Carefully turn the hash on to a large plate, then turn it over and slide back into the pan, so that the cooked side is facing up. Cook for a further 5 minutes until crisp and golden brown. Cut into wedges and serve warm.

CHEF'S TIP: For a quick fishy alternative, replace the pancetta with a small tin of cooked salmon. Simply drain it, flake it up and add to the grated potato with the salad onions and the salt and pepper.

Baconeese corn muffins

These muffins make a super breakfast served warm from the oven with a dollop of butter or soft cheese, or wrapped in a paper napkin and eaten on the go.

PREPARATION: 15 minutes COOKING TIME: 20 minutes

MAKES 8

100 g (4 oz) smoked streaky bacon, roughly chopped

50 g (2 oz) butter

300 g (11 oz) plain flour

2 teaspoons baking powder

25g (1 oz) cornmeal

1 teaspoon caster sugar

1 teaspoon salt

120 g (4½ oz) Cheddar, finely diced

1 egg, beaten

300 ml (½ pint) milk

METHOD

1 Pre-heat the oven to 200°C/400°F/Gas 6. Line a muffin tin with paper cases, or cut parchment into 8 x 15 cm (6 inch) circles and push them into the tin.

2 Cook the bacon in a non-stick frying-pan for 3–4 minutes until golden. Drain on kitchen paper. Add the butter to the pan, remove from the heat and leave to melt.

3 Sift the flour and baking powder into a large bowl and stir in the cornmeal, sugar, salt, cooked bacon and three quarters of the cheese. Crack the egg into a separate bowl and whisk in the milk and melted butter.

4 Stir the liquid into the dry ingredients, taking care not to over-mix. Divide the mixture between the paper cases, scatter over the reserved cheese and bake for 20 minutes or so until well risen and just firm.

5 Transfer to a wire rack, and allow to cool slightly – if you can wait, that is.

Pesto-rippled scrambled eggs

This is absolutely delicious, and the rippled effect comes not only from the pesto, but also from the egg yolks and whites being mixed together. But, be warned, it's worth sharing the finished dish with your partner as it contains raw garlic, which can have quite a long-lasting effect.

PREPARATION: 15 minutes COOKING TIME: 5 minutes

SERVES 2

1 small garlic clove, roughly chopped

1 tablespoon toasted pine nuts

15 g packet of fresh basil

1 tablespoon freshly grated Parmesan, plus extra to serve

2–3 tablespoons olive oil

large knob of butter

4 large eggs

salt and freshly ground black pepper

hot, buttered, toasted bread or bagels, to serve

METHOD

1 Place the garlic and pine nuts in a mini food processor and blitz until finely chopped. Add the basil and Parmesan and blitz again until well blended. Add the oil and some salt and pepper and pulse until well combined.

2 Heat the butter in a small pan and crack in the eggs, season, then leave to set for 2 minutes. With a wooden spoon, stir very gently so the eggs begin to set in clumps of white and yellow. Before the eggs have completely set, lightly stir in the pesto.

3 Pile on to the hot toast or bagels, scatter over the Parmesan and serve immediately.

Pesto-rippled scrambled eggs

Portabello mushroom open-top toast

Portabello mushrooms have a great firm texture and full flavour, making them ideal for cooking and pairing with other flavoursome ingredients such as garlicky soft cheese. Great for brunch – even better as a late-night snack.

PREPARATION: 10 minutes COOKING TIME: 10 minutes

SERVES 2

1 tablespoon olive oil

4 large Portabello mushrooms, about 50 g (2 oz) each

6 cherry tomatoes, halved

1 x 80 g pack garlic and herb soft cheese

salt and freshly ground black pepper

2 thick slices of hot, buttered toast, to serve

chives, to garnish

METHOD

1 Heat the oil in a large frying-pan, add the mushrooms, gill-side up and season lightly. Place 3 cherry tomato halves in each cap and dot over the soft cheese. Cook gently for 5 minutes over a low heat. Meanwhile, pre-heat the grill to medium.

2 Place the frying-pan under the grill for 2–3 minutes until the cheese is bubbling. Place two stuffed mushrooms on top of each slice of toast, garnish with chives and serve.

Portabello mushroom open-top toast

Posh eggy-bread BLT

For a quick snack or a truly indulgent breakfast, this is absolutely perfect – especially with a squirt of tomato ketchup or brown sauce on the side.

PREPARATION: 10 minutes COOKING TIME: 10 minutes

SERVES 1

2 tablespoons olive oil

2 slices smoked back bacon

1 plum tomato, sliced lengthways

1 large egg

2 tablespoons milk

2 slices white bread

small handful of watercress

1 tablespoon mayonnaise

salt and freshly ground black pepper

METHOD

1 Splash a little oil into a large, non-stick frying-pan. When hot, add the bacon and tomato slices. Cook over a high heat for a couple of minutes until the tomatoes are softened and a little browned and the bacon is done to your liking, then transfer to a plate. Remove the frying-pan from the heat and wipe clean with kitchen paper.

2 In a shallow bowl (I like to use a soup bowl) beat together the egg, milk and some salt and pepper.

3 Make a sandwich using the two slices of bread, add the bacon, tomato, watercress and mayonnaise. Press firmly together, then place the sandwich in the egg mixture. Leave for a few minutes, turning once or twice until all the egg mixture has been absorbed.

4 Add the remaining oil to the pan and return to the heat. Cook the sandwich for 3–4 minutes on each side until puffed and golden brown. Serve immediately.

Pineapple and coconut smoothie

What a great way to start the day! If you don't have time to skin your pineapple, you can buy one ready prepared; it can save loads of time in the morning rush.

PREPARATION: 10 minutes

SERVES 2-4

1 medium pineapple

1 banana

1 x 200 ml carton coconut cream

METHOD

1 Cut the skin off the pineapple and discard, then roughly chop the flesh. Pass through an electric juicer.

2 Peel and mash the banana, then mix with a little of the coconut cream until smooth. Transfer to a large, ice-filled jug with the remaining coconut cream and the pineapple juice. Stir very well together until blended and frothy then pour into 4 chilled glasses and serve.

CHEF'S TIP: Try substituting a wedge of watermelon for the pineapple.

Chorizo chowder

A warming, wintry soup, this makes a really satisfying supper or weekend lunch. Make sure you buy whole chorizo sausages and slice them yourself, as the packets of ready sliced chorizo that you can buy are too thin for this soup.

PREPARATION: 15 minutes COOKING TIME: 25 minutes

SERVES 4

knob of butter

1 small onion, finely chopped

4 garlic cloves, chopped

500 g (1 lb 2 oz) floury potatoes such as Maris Piper or King Edward, cubed

1 leek, thinly sliced

1 teaspoon cayenne

1 litre (1¾ pints) of vegetable stock

250 g (9 oz) chorizo sausage, cut into 1 cm (½ inch) wide slices, or 1 cm (½ inch) dice

salt and freshly ground black pepper

crusty bread, to serve

METHOD

1 Heat the butter in a large pan and cook the onion, garlic and potatoes for 5 minutes until lightly golden. Add the leek and cayenne and cook for a further 1 minute.

2 Add the stock, bring to the boil and simmer for 20 minutes until the potatoes are very soft and beginning to break up into the soup.

3 Using a potato masher, roughly mash the potatoes into the soup. Stir in the chorizo and simmer gently for 5 minutes until the orange-coloured oil from the chorizo rises to the surface of the soup. Check the seasoning, ladle into bowls and garnish with a sprig of flat-leaf parsley. Serve with lots of crusty bread for mopping up.

Chorizo chowder

Chickpea, spinach and sweet potato soup

This is a lovely, hearty, warming soup that everyone adores, especially my veggie friends. Pair it with crusty bread for a cosy supper.

PREPARATION: 10 minutes COOKING TIME: 20 minutes

SERVES 4

2 tablespoons sunflower oil

1 onion, finely chopped

1 sweet potato, diced

1 garlic clove, thinly sliced

1 teaspoon cumin seeds

400 g can chickpeas, drained

2 tomatoes, roughly chopped

1 teaspoon honey

750 ml (1¼ pints) hot vegetable stock

225 g (8 oz) young leaf spinach

salt and freshly ground black pepper

METHOD

1 Heat the oil in a large pan and cook the onion, sweet potato and garlic for 5 minutes, stirring until beginning to turn golden. Add the cumin seeds and cook for 30 seconds. Stir in the chickpeas, tomatoes and honey and cook for 1–2 minutes until the tomatoes begin to soften.

2 Stir in the hot stock, bring to the boil, then cover and simmer for 10 minutes until the sweet potato is tender.

3 Stir in the spinach and cook for 1 minute, stirring until the spinach wilts. Season to taste, then ladle into bowls and serve.

Hot Bloody Mary soup

The combination of tomato, vodka and chilli works brilliantly in the classic cocktail and it's every bit as good in this dazzling soup – it certainly packs a punch. It's essential that you add the horseradish, sherry and vodka when the soup is off the boil, otherwise you'll impair the lovely flavour.

PREPARATION: 20 minutes COOKING TIME: 40 minutes

SERVES 4

1 kg (2¼ lb) ripe tomatoes, halved

2 red chillies, halved and seeded

2 teaspoons caster sugar

2 tablespoons olive oil

750 ml (1¼ pint) vegetable stock

1 tablespoon tomato purée

2 teaspoons horseradish sauce

2 tablespoons dry sherry

4 tablespoons vodka

4 small celery stalks, with leaves

celery salt, or salt and freshly ground black pepper

4 thin lemon slices, to garnish

METHOD

1 Pre-heat the oven to 200°C/400°F/Gas 4. Place the tomatoes cut-side up in a large roasting tin with the chillies and sprinkle over the sugar and some salt and pepper. Drizzle over the olive oil and roast for 30 minutes until softened and nicely browned.

2 Purée the roasted tomatoes in a blender with a little stock until smooth. For a really smooth soup, pass the purée through a sieve into a large pan, otherwise, transfer straight to the pan. Stir in the remaining stock and the tomato purée and heat gently through, without boiling.

3 Stir in the horseradish, sherry and vodka and check the seasoning. Place a celery stalk in each of four bowls and ladle over the soup. Grind over black pepper, float a slice of lemon on each and serve.

Asian salmon laksa

This Asian soup is substantial enough to serve as a smart supper, but is also lovely as a dinner-party starter, providing it's not followed by too heavy a main course. I like to use pak choi, but you could use spinach.

PREPARATION: 20 minutes   COOKING TIME: 10 minutes

SERVES 4

300 g (11 oz) salmon fillet

juice of 2 limes

100 g (4 oz) rice noodles

1 tablespoon vegetable oil

2.5 cm (1 inch) piece root ginger, finely chopped

2 garlic cloves, finely chopped

1 shallot, finely chopped

450 ml (¾ pint) hot vegetable stock

400 g can coconut milk

1 lemon grass stalk

2 teaspoons Thai red curry paste

200 g (7 oz) pak choi, halved or quartered if large

1 tablespoon soy sauce

1 small red chilli, sliced to garnish

METHOD

1   Boil a kettle of water. Cut the salmon widthways into 1-cm (½-inch) wide slices (you should get roughly 12 slices out of a fillet of this size). Place in a bowl and squeeze over the lime juice; set aside for 20 minutes.

2   Meanwhile, place the noodles in a large bowl, cover with the boiling water and set aside.

3   Heat the oil in a large pan or wok, throw in the ginger, garlic and shallots and cook for 3–4 minutes until softened. Pour in the stock and coconut milk, then bruise the lemon grass stalk with a rolling pin – a quick bash or two should do it – and add to the pan with the curry paste. Stir well. Then, bring the soup to the boil, reduce the heat and simmer very gently for 5 minutes.

4   Add the salmon, pak choi and soy sauce and simmer for another 2–3 minutes until the pak choi is tender, but still crunchy.

5   Drain the noodles and divide between four bowls. Ladle over the soup, then float a chilli ring or two in each bowl. Serve immediately.

Asian salmon laksa

Shredded chicken
and lemon grass soup

This is a low-fat, delicate, aromatic broth. It makes a lovely light supper or can serve up to six as a starter. For this soup I use the whole chilli, including the seeds, which, when blended with the other flavours, gives it a wonderful kick. Make sure you use whole thighs with the bones in as this contributes greatly to the flavour of the broth.

PREPARATION: 10 minutes COOKING TIME: 35 minutes

SERVES 4

6 whole chicken thighs

2 lemon grass stalks

2 kaffir lime leaves

2 garlic cloves, halved

1 red chilli, roughly chopped

4 cm (1½ inch) piece root ginger, thickly sliced

juice of 1 lime

4 tablespoons light soy sauce

1 bunch salad onions, thinly sliced

1 tablespoon fresh coriander leaves

METHOD

1 Remove the skin from the chicken thighs and discard; place the thighs in a large pan. Bruise the lemon grass with a rolling pin and crumple the lime leaves in the palm of your hand. Place in the pan with the garlic, chilli, including the seeds, and ginger and 1.5 litres (2½ pints) water. Bring to the boil and simmer for 30 minutes until the chicken is cooked right through.

2 Strain the stock into a clean pan then, using 2 forks, shred the meat off the bones. Return the chicken to the pan with the fresh lime juice, soy sauce and sliced salad onions. Heat through gently and, when steaming hot, ladle into bowls. Loosely scatter over the coriander leaves and serve.

CHEF'S TIP: This soup is naturally quite low in fat, but for pretty presentation and a little extra flavour, try drizzling a splash of chilli or sesame oil over the surface of each serving.

Curried parsnip soup

I like to serve this soup with those delicious root-vegetable crisps you can buy now. Just drop a handful into the centre of each bowlful.

PREPARATION: 15 minutes COOKING TIME: 45 minutes

SERVES 6

4 large parsnips, cubed, about 750 g (1½ lb)

6 whole garlic cloves, skinned

4 cm (1½ inch) piece root ginger, roughly chopped

1 tablespoon vegetable oil

1.2 litres (2 pints) hot vegetable stock

400 ml can coconut milk

1 tablespoon Thai red curry paste

salt and freshly ground black pepper

1 tablespoon chopped fresh coriander

root vegetable crisps, to serve

METHOD

1 Pre-heat the oven to 200°C/400°F/Gas 6. Place the parsnips, garlic and ginger in a large, deep roasting tin, drizzle over the oil, season with salt and pepper and roast for 20 minutes until golden.

2 Pour in half the stock, the coconut milk and curry paste and return to the oven for a further 20 minutes until the vegetables are tender.

3 Transfer to a liquidizer and blend until creamy and smooth. Add the remaining hot stock and the coriander and check the seasoning. Ladle into warm bowls and serve with the root vegetable crisps.

CHEF'S TIP: This soup is served warm but not piping hot. If you prefer, it can be warmed through a little further in a pan on the stove before serving. It can also be chilled and gently reheated for serving later.

Chinese crisp-fried
salt-and-pepper squid

This is one of my all-time favourite Chinese dishes and it's surprisingly easy to make. I think baby squid are best for this recipe as they cook quickly and are lovely and tender. Baby squid can be bought from larger supermarkets, or try your local fishmonger – if you ask him nicely he might score them for you, too.

PREPARATION: 15 minutes COOKING TIME: 10 minutes

SERVES 4

300 g (11 oz) young squid, each about 4–6 cm (1¾–2½ inches) long, cleaned

vegetable oil for deep-frying

1 tablespoon sea salt

1 tablespoon black peppercorns

75 g (3 oz) cornflour

1 red chilli, very thinly sliced, seeds and all

2 salad onions, cut into 1 cm (½ inch) pieces

soy sauce and lemon wedges, to serve

METHOD

1 Slit each squid body open along one side with a sharp knife then score the inside of each in a criss-cross pattern. Set aside with the tentacles.

2 Heat 5 cm (2 inches) of vegetable oil in the base of a wok or deep frying-pan.

3 Place the sea salt and peppercorns in a pestle and mortar and crush coarsely together. Stir into the cornflour, then toss with the squid to coat – you might find it easier to place the ingredients in a large plastic bag and shake well together.

4 Cook the chillies and salad onions in the hot oil for 30 seconds then scoop them out with a mesh spoon and drain on kitchen paper. Cook the squid body and tentacles in the pan for 2 minutes until it rolls up and turns crisp and lightly golden – you may need to do this in batches so the oil stays hot. Drain on kitchen paper.

5 Transfer the squid to a plate, scatter over the crispy chilli and salad onions and serve with soy sauce for drizzling and lemon wedges for squeezing over.

Chinese crisp-fried salt-and-pepper squid

Crispy noodle-wrapped prawns
with rice-wine dipping sauce

This is a very stylish starter. It's ideal for a dinner party menu, followed by Warm Oriental Duck and Mango Salad (page 250) then Srikhand with Iced Mango Shards (page 309). Try to get your prawns from a Chinese grocer or a local fishmonger, as the ones in the supermarket are too tiddly for this dish.

PREPARATION: 20 minutes COOKING TIME: 10 minutes

SERVES 4

75 g (3 oz) dried, fine, Chinese egg noodles

1 small mango, skinned, stoned and thinly sliced

12 large, raw, shell-on, headless prawns, each about 8 cm (3¼ inches) long

salt

vegetable oil for deep frying

FOR THE DIPPING SAUCE

5 tablespoons rice or white wine vinegar

3 tablespoons caster sugar

1 red bird's-eye chilli, very thinly sliced, seeds and all

sprigs of fresh coriander and wedges of lime, to serve

METHOD

1 Begin by making the dipping sauce: place the vinegar and sugar in a small pan and bring to the boil, stirring until the sugar dissolves. Remove from the heat, add the sliced chilli and leave to cool completely. If you want to get ahead, the sauce can be made a day or two before you need it, then kept covered in the fridge.

2 Cook the egg noodles in a pan of boiling water according to packet instructions. Drain well, then cool in cold water and drain again. Gently heat 5 cm (2 inches) of oil in a deep pan.

3 Shell the prawns, leaving the tail section intact. Pass a short bamboo skewer through the prawn from top to tail. Place a slice of mango on each prawn and season with a little salt. Gather about 6 strands of noodle and wrap them around the prawn to secure together the prawn and the mango. Repeat to make 12 prawn sticks.

4 Test the oil temperature with a piece of noodle: it should turn crisp and golden in about 1 minute. Cook the prawns in batches for 2–3 minutes until the noodles are crisp and the prawns pink. Drain on kitchen paper and serve hot with small bowls of the dipping sauce. You may choose to slide the prawns off the sticks before serving, or leave them on. Decorate with sprigs of coriander and wedges of lime, to serve.

Crispy noodle-wrapped prawns with rice-wine dipping sauce

Seared scallops with
endive and Roquefort

If you enjoy seafood that's rich and delicious, this is undoubtedly one of the finest dishes on offer. I always think Queen scallops work best in this dish – your fishmonger should be able to get them for you. If you're daunted by the prospect of cleaning them, your fishmonger will probably do this for you too.

PREPARATION: 10 minutes COOKING TIME: 5 minutes

SERVES 4

2 small heads chicory

12 small scallops, shelled

2 tablespoons olive oil

1 teaspoon walnut oil

juice of half a lime

100 g (4 oz) Roquefort, crumbled into 1 cm (½ inch) pieces

2 tablespoons snipped fresh chives

salt and freshly ground black pepper

METHOD

1 Break open the chicory and place 3 leaves on each of 4 plates.

2 Brush the scallops with a little of the olive oil. Cook in a hot, non-stick frying-pan for 1 minute on each side until golden.

3 Place a scallop on each leaf. Whisk together the remaining olive oil, walnut oil, lime juice and some salt and pepper. Top each leaf with a cube or two of Roquefort and a scattering of chives, then drizzle over the dressing and serve while the scallops are still just warm.

Vietnamese-style pork
in lettuce-leaf cups

Now, here's a classic Oriental dish that's surprisingly easy to make at home. What's even better is that you can prepare it the day before and then, just before your guests arrive, assemble the dish in a matter of minutes. It's perfect to serve up for a dinner party, or just to enjoy with the family.

PREPARATION: 15 minutes + cooling time COOKING TIME: 10 minutes

SERVES 4

1 tablespoon vegetable oil

1 shallot, finely chopped

2 garlic cloves, finely chopped

1 red chilli, seeded and finely chopped

250 g (9 oz) minced pork

1 teaspoon Chinese five spice

220 g can water chestnuts, drained and chopped

1 tablespoon Thai fish sauce (nam pla)

2 tablespoons light soy sauce

1 tablespoon clear honey

2 Little Gem lettuce hearts

75 g (3 oz) bean sprouts

fresh coriander leaves, to garnish

METHOD

1 Heat the oil in a large pan and cook the shallot and garlic for 2 minutes. Add the chilli, pork and five spice and cook for a further 5 minutes. Stir in the water chestnuts, fish sauce, soy sauce and honey and warm through gently, stirring until the pork is cooked through. Allow to cool then chill for at least 20 minutes.

2 Separate the lettuce leaves and place 12 on a large serving platter. Stir the bean sprouts into the minced pork then spoon into the lettuce leaves. Garnish with coriander leaves and serve.

Crispy Parma ham
and asparagus salad

This is a gorgeous main-meal salad. When in season, during May, try to use delicious home-grown English asparagus.

PREPARATION: 10 minutes COOKING TIME: 20 minutes

SERVES 4

6 eggs

250 g (9 oz) asparagus

25 g (1 oz) butter

squeeze of fresh lemon juice

8 slices Parma ham, about 85 g (3¼ oz)

salt and freshly ground black pepper

Parmesan shavings, to serve

METHOD

1 Cook the eggs in a pan of boiling water for exactly 8 minutes. Sit a steamer or colander over the eggs, put in the asparagus, cover and cook for 4–5 minutes until just tender – alternatively, cook in a pan of boiling water for 2–3 minutes.

2 Drain the eggs and asparagus and cool under cold water.

3 Melt the butter in a small pan then, with a wire whisk, beat in some lemon juice and salt and pepper to taste.

4 Heat a ridged griddle pan or heavy, non-stick frying-pan. Cook the slices of Parma ham, two at a time in the hot pan for 30 seconds on each side. Set aside on kitchen paper. Cook the asparagus in the hot pan (making good use of the fat left from the Parma ham) for 2–3 minutes to give light bar-marks.

5 Shell and halve the eggs and arrange on four plates with the asparagus, topped with the crispy Parma ham. Drizzle over the lemon-butter dressing. Scatter over the shaved Parmesan and top with a good grind of black pepper. A glass or two of chilled white wine is the perfect accompaniment to this dish.

Crispy Parma ham and asparagus salad

Beef satay chilli sticks

These tasty morsels are the perfect way to start off a dinner party or to serve with drinks – they're never around for very long. I like to hand them round to my mates when we're watching the footie on TV – the satay sticks get a bigger cheer than any goals being scored, except when they're scored by Arsenal.

PREPARATION: 15 minutes + marinating time COOKING TIME: 5 minutes

SERVES 4

500 g (1 lb 2 oz) trimmed 2.5 cm (1 inch) rump steak

4 tablespoons light soy sauce

2 teaspoons brown sugar

1 teaspoon vinegar

coriander leaves or shredded salad onions, to garnish

FOR THE SAUCE

50 g pack dry-roasted peanuts

1 garlic clove

200 ml carton coconut cream

juice of 1 lime

1 tablespoon light soy sauce

pinch of crushed chilli flakes

METHOD

1 You will need 8 bamboo skewers for this recipe. Before you start, soak them in hot water for approximately 20 minutes.

2 Slice the steak lengthways into 5 mm (¼ inch) thick strips. When you lay them flat, they will be 2.5 cm (1 inch) wide and about 12 cm (4¾ inches) long, depending upon the length of your steak. Place the steak strips into a bowl with the soy sauce, sugar and vinegar. Stir well together and leave to marinate for at least 15 minutes and up to 2 hours.

3 Meanwhile, make the satay sauce: place the peanuts and garlic in a food processor and whizz until very finely chopped. Add the coconut cream and whizz again until well blended. Pour into a small pan and heat gently for 3–4 minutes until the sauce darkens and thickens slightly. Add the soy sauce and lime juice to taste, then remove from the heat.

4 Thread the steak on to the bamboo skewers – make a concertina with each strip so that the skewer passes through several times – and place on a foil-lined baking sheet. Cook under a hot grill for 2–3 minutes on each side until browned but still pink in the centre. You can cook them for longer if you like your steak better done.

5 Pour the warm satay sauce into a serving bowl and sprinkle with the crushed chillies. Arrange the beef sticks on a platter, garnish with coriander or salad onions and serve with the sauce for dipping.

Quick chicken liver and
tarragon paté

Forget about paté that takes ages to cook in a water bath. This recipe is incredibly simple and tastes fabulous. Just cook, purée, set and serve. It's as easy as that!

PREPARATION: 20 minutes + chilling time COOKING TIME: 10 minutes

SERVES 6

150 g (5 oz) butter, at room temperature

225 g (8 oz) chicken livers

2 tablespoons brandy

2 garlic cloves, roughly chopped

1 tablespoon chopped fresh tarragon

142 ml carton double cream

salt and freshly ground black pepper

hot, buttered toast, to serve

TO GARNISH

50 g (2 oz) butter

12 fresh tarragon leaves

METHOD

1 Melt a large knob of the butter in a large frying-pan and cook the chicken livers for 3–4 minutes on each side until well browned but still slightly pink in the centre.

2 Place in a food processor and whizz until smooth. Remove the pan from the heat, add the brandy and swirl round to gather up the pan juices. Add to the food processor with the garlic, tarragon and the remaining butter and whizz again until well blended.

3 Add some salt and pepper followed by the cream and process again until well mixed. Spoon into 6 ramekins, smoothing the surface level, and leave to cool completely.

4 To finish off, melt the butter and pour over the surface of the paté. Drop in a few tarragon leaves as decoration.

5 Cover with cling film and chill for at least a few hours, but up to a day or two. Serve straight from the fridge with hot, buttered toast, or melba toast if you're feeling posh.

Chilli crab linguine with vodka

A delicious, delicate dish this, I often serve it up as a simple supper for my wife Clare and myself, once the kids are tucked up in bed. I tend to use canned crab, but if you can get fresh, all the better. If you are feeding youngsters, skip the chilli and the vodka, but I'd recommend that you keep this dish strictly for adults.

PREPARATION: 10 minutes COOKING TIME: 15 minutes

SERVES 2

175 g (6 oz) dried linguine

1 tablespoon olive oil

1 shallot, finely chopped

1 small garlic clove, finely chopped

1 red chilli, seeded and finely chopped

2 ripe tomatoes, roughly chopped

1 tablespoon vodka (optional)

170 g can white crab meat, drained

2 tablespoons chopped fresh flat-leaf parsley

salt and freshly ground black pepper

METHOD

1 Cook the pasta in a large pan of boiling, salted water according to packet instructions.

2 Meanwhile, heat the olive oil in a frying-pan and cook the shallot, garlic and chilli over a low to medium heat for 2–3 minutes until beginning to soften, but not brown. Add the tomatoes, increase the heat and cook for 4–5 minutes until pulpy.

3 Now stir in the vodka, if using, followed by the crab meat, and stir gently together. Season to taste.

4 Drain the pasta well and return to the pan. Add the sauce and the chopped parsley and stir loosely together. Divide between bowls and top with a good grinding of black pepper.

CHEF'S TIP: Don't be tempted to get out the Parmesan – it really doesn't suit the flavour of the crab.

Chilli crab linguine with vodka

Grilled mackerel
with shallot and coriander pickle

Mackerel is a lovely oily fish and its flavour contrasts wonderfully with the sharpness of the quick pickle that's served with it. I cook these under the grill, but they're even more fabulous cooked alfresco over hot coals in the great outdoors. I like to serve this with Spice-roasted Butternut Squash (page 301) and a simple green salad.

PREPARATION: 10 minutes + marinating time COOKING TIME: 10 minutes

SERVES 4

4 x 300–350 g (11–12 oz) whole, cleaned mackerel

1 tablespoon olive oil

sea salt and coarsely ground black pepper

FOR THE PICKLE

2 shallots

2 cornichons or small pickled gherkins

4 tablespoons red wine vinegar

3 tablespoons caster sugar

¼ teaspoon table salt

1 teaspoon yellow mustard seeds

15 g packet fresh coriander, roughly chopped

METHOD

1 Begin by making the pickle: halve and peel the shallots, then slice them lengthways as thinly as possible. Thinly slice the cornichons and place in a bowl with the shallots, vinegar, sugar, salt and mustard seeds. Set aside for 20 minutes.

2 Meanwhile, diagonally cut 3 deep slashes on each side of the fish. Smear with the olive oil then season with salt and pepper. Heat the grill to medium. Place the fish on a foil-lined baking sheet and cook under the grill for 4–5 minutes on each side until the skin is crisp and brown and the flesh is cooked.

3 Stir the coriander leaves into the shallot mixture and leave for 2–3 minutes. Transfer the mackerel to serving plates and spoon over the pickle.

CHEF'S TIP: Crusty fresh bread would be ideal to serve with this, so that you can mop up all those juices.

Gruyère cracker-crusted haddock

The crackers add a fantastic crunch to this tasty fish dish.

PREPARATION: 10 minutes COOKING TIME: 10 minutes

SERVES 4

75 g (3 oz) water biscuits or cream crackers

75 g (3 oz) finely grated Gruyère

½ teaspoon cayenne

2 tablespoons chopped fresh parsley

2 tablespoons olive oil

4 x 150 g (5 oz) skinless, boneless haddock fillets

salt and freshly ground black pepper

METHOD

1 Crumble the crackers into a food processor with the Gruyère, cayenne and parsley and blitz until well blended. Add 1 tablespoon of the olive oil and some seasoning and pulse again until well blended.

2 Heat the remaining oil in a large frying-pan and cook the haddock for 2–3 minutes until nearly cooked through. Sprinkle the cracker-crumb mixture over the top of the fillets, pressing down firmly with the fingertips.

3 Pre-heat the grill to medium. Place the pan under the grill for 4–5 minutes until the fish is completely cooked through and the crumb topping is golden brown.

CHEF'S TIP: Gruyère has a full flavour and stretchy quality when melted. It can be substituted in this dish with tasty Jarlsberg or milder Emmenthal.

Smoked haddock, leek and rösti-pot pie

Haddock and leeks make a wonderful flavour combination and they're finished off beautifully with a crunchy potato and Cheddar cheese topping.

PREPARATION: 25 minutes COOKING TIME: 25 minutes

SERVES 4–6

500 g (1 lb 2 oz) smoked haddock fillet

300 ml (½ pint) milk

25 g (1 oz) butter

2 large leeks, sliced

25 g (1 oz) plain flour

2 teaspoons wholegrain mustard

250 g carton mascarpone

3 hard boiled eggs, quartered

1 large floury potato, about 250 g (9 oz), such as Maris Piper or King Edward

75 g (3 oz) coarsely grated mature Cheddar

salt and freshly ground black pepper

METHOD

1 Place the fish in a heatproof dish. Bring the milk to the boil in a small pan and pour over the fish; set aside for 5 minutes.

2 Pre-heat the oven to 200°C/400°F/Gas 6. Heat the butter in a large pan and cook the sliced leeks for 3 minutes until softened. Stir in the flour and cook for 1 minute, stirring continuously. Strain the milk from the fish into the pan and stir well.

3 Bring to the boil and continue stirring until thickened. Now add the mustard and mascarpone, mixing until warmed through and well blended. Add salt and pepper to taste and remove from the heat.

4 Skin the fish, then cut or break the flesh into chunks and transfer to a 2 litre (3½ pint) heatproof dish. Add the quartered eggs, then pour over the leek sauce, stirring lightly to mix everything together.

5 Peel then coarsely grate the potato and mix with the cheese and some freshly ground black pepper. Scatter this mixture evenly over the top of the pie then bake for 25–30 minutes until the topping is golden brown. Serve straight from the oven.

CHEF'S TIP: The potato will turn grey when exposed to the air so make sure you grate it at the last minute and bake the pie as soon as the topping is on.

Portuguese string-tied, stuffed sardines

Ask your fishmonger to bone the sardines for you while keeping them whole – it's very easy to do. Simply serve with a plain salad for a lovely summery supper or lunch.

PREPARATION: 20 minutes COOKING TIME: 10 minutes

SERVES 4

2 tablespoons olive oil

1 shallot, finely chopped

2 garlic cloves, finely chopped

1 teaspoon chopped capers

4 tablespoons chopped fresh parsley

100 g (4 oz) fresh white breadcrumbs

grated rind and juice of 1 lemon

12 x 50–75 g (2–3 oz) whole sardines, boned if possible

3 mild red chillies, quartered lengthways and seeded

salt and freshly ground black pepper

METHOD

1 Heat 1 tablespoon of the oil in a large pan and cook the shallot and garlic for 4–5 minutes until softened and golden. Stir in the capers, parsley, breadcrumbs, lemon rind and juice and some salt and pepper.

2 Open out the sardines and place a tablespoon of the stuffing mixture into each cavity. Close the sardines to enclose the filling, then tie with string to secure.

3 Pre-heat the grill to high. Slip a strip of chilli under the strings of each fish then brush with a little olive oil. Season with salt and pepper then cook under the grill or in a non-stick frying-pan for 3–4 minutes on each side until cooked through and a little charred. Serve warm with salad.

Sesame-salt roast sea bass
with ginger soy dressing

This is a really glamorous and colourful dish. Apart from some careful chopping, it's really easy to prepare. Serve it with my Simple Wok Noodles (page 305).

PREPARATION: 15 minutes   COOKING TIME: 30 minutes

SERVES 4

2 tablespoons sesame seeds

2 teaspoons sea salt

1 sea bass, about 1.25–1.5kg (2¾–3¼ lb)

1–2 tablespoons sunflower oil

2 cm (¾ inch) piece root ginger, shredded

1 garlic clove, finely chopped

1 red chilli, seeded and shredded

4 tablespoons soy sauce

2 teaspoons white vinegar or rice vinegar

2 teaspoons sesame oil

4 salad onions, shredded

handful of fresh coriander

salt and freshly ground black pepper

lime wedges, to serve

METHOD

1 Pre-heat the oven to 200°C/400°F/Gas 6. Mix together the sesame seeds and salt. Season the cavity of the fish then make 3 diagonal slashes across each side of the bass so it cooks evenly.

2 Transfer the fish to a large roasting tin and brush with a little oil. Scatter over the sesame salt and roast for 25–30 minutes until the fish is cooked and lightly golden.

3 Meanwhile, splash a little sunflower oil into a small pan and cook the ginger, garlic and chilli for 2 minutes, without browning. Add the soy sauce, vinegar and sesame oil and remove from the heat.

4 When the fish is cooked, transfer to a large serving platter. Pour over the ginger dressing, then scatter over the salad onions and coriander leaves. Serve immediately with lime wedges for squeezing over.

Sesame-salt roast sea bass with ginger soy dressing

Cold poached salmon
with cucumber and crème fraîche sauce

This is a really simple but very elegant summer dish. It's light and healthy, so I choose to use low-fat crème fraîche for the sauce. Serve with boiled, new, Jersey potatoes.

PREPARATION: 15 minutes + cooling time COOKING TIME: 5 minutes

SERVES 4

4 peppercorns

6 fresh dill sprigs, plus extra to serve

1 lemon, thinly sliced

450 ml (¾ pint) boiling water

4 x 175 g (6 oz) salmon fillets

FOR THE SAUCE

1 mini cucumber, roughly chopped

2 fresh dill sprigs

200 ml carton low-fat crème fraîche

salt and freshly ground black pepper

METHOD

1 Place the peppercorns, dill and four lemon slices (reserve the remaining slices for the garnish) in a large sauté pan and pour in the boiling water. Add the salmon, cover with a tight-fitting lid and cook for 5 minutes. Turn off the heat and leave the salmon to cool completely in the water – this should cook it perfectly. Remove from the pan then transfer to a plate, cover and chill until ready to serve.

2 To make the sauce, place the cucumber and dill in a food processor and whizz until smooth. Add the crème fraîche and some salt and pepper and pulse to make a smooth, pourable sauce.

3 To serve, place a salmon fillet on 4 plates and pour over the sauce. Garnish each with a slice of lemon and sprig of dill.

Souffléd smoked salmon
and tarragon omelette

This delicious soufflette makes a lovely main course for one, or a posh breakfast for two – beats boring old scrambled eggs and smoked salmon hands down.

PREPARATION: 10 minutes COOKING TIME: 7 minutes

SERVES 1

3 eggs, separated

1 small garlic clove, crushed

1 tablespoon chopped fresh tarragon, plus a sprig to garnish

50 g (2 oz) smoked salmon trimmings, roughly chopped

1 teaspoon olive oil

1 tablespoon freshly grated Parmesan

salt and freshly ground black pepper

METHOD

1 In a large bowl, mix together the egg yolks, garlic and tarragon, and season. Stir in the smoked salmon.

2 In a separate bowl, whisk the egg whites until they form soft peaks, then fold into the egg yolk mixture.

3 Heat the olive oil in a 20 cm (8 in) non-stick frying-pan and pour in the egg mixture. Cook gently over a low to medium heat for 2–3 minutes until golden brown underneath. You can check how brown the omelette is by gently lifting the edge with a knife.

4 Pre-heat the grill to medium. Sprinkle the Parmesan over the omelette and pop under the grill for 3–4 minutes until golden and set. Slide on to a plate and serve.

CHEF'S TIP: Pile rocket or watercress into the centre of the omelette and sprinkle with balsamic or olive oil for a great tasting variation.

Creamy salmon spaghetti

It's amazing how such a simple dish can turn out so stylishly. I've chosen to use the tail fillet of salmon as it's thinner than the thick fillets from the middle of the fish, which means it'll cook more quickly and it's more economical, too. I know I always say don't add Parmesan to fishy pasta, but in this case, believe me, it's delicious.

PREPARATION: 5 minutes COOKING TIME: 15 minutes

SERVES 4

300 g (11 oz) spaghetti

300 ml carton double cream

2 garlic cloves

2 teaspoons tomato purée

250 g (9 oz) skinless, boneless salmon tail fillet

4 tablespoons freshly grated Parmesan, plus extra, to serve

salt and freshly ground black pepper

METHOD

1 Cook the pasta in a large pan of boiling, salted water according to the packet instructions.

2 Meanwhile, pour the cream into a small pan and crush in the garlic cloves. Stir in the tomato purée and heat gently. Cut the fish widthways into 1cm (½ inch) wide strips and, once the cream is hot, stir in the salmon and remove from the heat (the heat from the cream will cook the fish in about 3–4 minutes). Add salt and pepper to taste.

3 Drain the pasta and return to the pan. Stir in the salmon mixture and the Parmesan, then divide between bowls. Pass round more Parmesan for sprinkling over.

Tuna and parsley tagliatelle

This is one of those dishes that I can always knock up when I haven't had time to get in the shopping – it's a real store-cupboard saviour and it's very tasty too. Like most fishy pasta dishes, hold the Parmesan.

PREPARATION: 10 minutes COOKING TIME: 15 minutes

SERVES 2

200 g (7 oz) dried tagliatelle

3 tablespoons olive oil

1 small onion, finely chopped

2 garlic cloves, finely chopped

1 red chilli, seeded and finely chopped

250 g (9 oz) chestnut mushrooms, halved

185 g can tuna in spring water or brine, drained

4 tablespoons chopped fresh parsley

salt and freshly ground black pepper

METHOD

1   Cook the pasta in a large pan of boiling salted water, according to the packet instructions.

2   Meanwhile, heat 2 tablespoon of the oil in a large frying-pan and cook the onion, garlic and chilli for 2–3 minutes. Add the mushrooms and cook for a further 3–4 minutes until beginning to brown. Stir in the tuna and 2–3 tablespoons of boiling water from the pasta pan. Add salt and pepper to taste.

3   Drain the pasta well and return to the pan. Stir in the tuna mixture, the parsley and remaining tablespoon of olive oil. Divide between 2 bowls and serve topped with a good grinding of black pepper.

CHEF'S TIP: My wife likes a dollop of crème fraîche on top of her pasta, and I have to say it really does taste good.

Fresh charred tuna steak
with salsa verde

Oh, I love a bit of salsa verde. It translates simply as 'green sauce', and I vary it frequently to include my favourite flavourings (or whatever's in my store-cupboard). This version is fantastic with most plain grilled or fried fish and is a perfect match for a fresh tuna steak. I like it quite rough, so I prefer to chop it by hand, but you can give it a quick blitz in the blender if you prefer.

PREPARATION: 15 minutes COOKING TIME: 10 minutes

SERVES 4

2 anchovy fillets

1 tablespoon salted capers

1 green chilli, seeded and finely chopped

1 garlic clove, crushed

3 tablespoons chopped fresh parsley

1 tablespoon chopped fresh coriander

2 teaspoons Dijon mustard

4 tablespoons olive oil

1 tablespoon white wine vinegar

4 x 150–200 g (5–7 oz) tuna steaks

salt and freshly ground black pepper

METHOD

1 Place the anchovy fillets and capers on to a large board and, using a heavy knife, finely chop them. Place the chilli and garlic on top and chop again until finely minced.

2 Scrape into a bowl and stir in the herbs, mustard, 3 tablespoons of the oil and the vinegar. Season with black pepper and set aside.

3 Pre-heat a ridged griddle pan or heavy, non-stick frying-pan. Lightly brush the tuna with oil and season with salt and pepper. Cook for 3–4 minutes on each side until just cooked through but still a little pink in the centre. Transfer to 4 serving plates and spoon over the salsa. Serve immediately.

Fresh charred tuna steak with salsa verde *with* Fennel, orange and olive salad (page 304)

French-style roasted cod

This is a beautifully easy, rustic-style dish, packed with flavour. Serve at the table so your guests see it, still sizzling, in its roasting tin.

PREPARATION: 15 minutes COOKING TIME: 25 minutes

SERVES 4

450 g (1 lb) floury potatoes such as Maris Piper, peeled and cubed

1 garlic bulb

4 plum tomatoes

4 rosemary sprigs

3 tablespoons olive oil

4 x 150 g (5 oz) thick boneless cod fillets, skin on

4 tablespoons white wine

salt and freshly ground black pepper

handful of fresh basil leaves, to garnish

METHOD

1 Pre-heat the oven to 220°C/425°F/Gas 7. Cook the potatoes in a large pan of boiling water for 10 minutes until almost tender and starting to crumble slightly around the edges.

2 Drain the potatoes well and transfer to a large roasting tin. Break the garlic bulb and nestle the cloves between the potatoes. Roughly chop the tomatoes and scatter over the top with the rosemary. Season generously, then drizzle over 2 tablespoons of the olive oil. Roast for 15 minutes.

3 Add the cod fillets to the pan, allowing them to rest on top of the potatoes and tomatoes. Drizzle the remaining oil over the top, season the fish and cook for 5 minutes. Splash in the wine and cook for a further 5 minutes until the fish is just cooked.

4 Tear over the basil leaves and serve straight from the pan. Remember to remind your guests that they'll need to peel the cloves of garlic before they eat them.

French-style roasted cod

Oven-baked
mussel and cherry tomato risotto

This is a delightful supper dish. The combination of fresh mussels and a delicious, moist wine and herb-scented tomato risotto is perfect. You'll need to get hold of a large roasting tin and some strong, wide kitchen foil before you start.

PREPARATION: 15 minutes COOKING TIME: 45 minutes

SERVES 4

350 g (12 oz) cherry tomatoes

1 red onion, finely chopped

1 tablespoon olive oil

300 g (11 oz) risotto rice such as Arborio or Carnaroli

150 ml (¼ pint) white wine

750 ml (1¼ pints) hot vegetable stock

2 sprigs fresh rosemary

1 kg (2¼ lb) small, live mussels, cleaned

2 tablespoons chopped fresh parsley

salt and freshly ground black pepper

METHOD

1 Pre-heat the oven to 200°C/400°F/Gas 6. Place the cherry tomatoes in a large roasting tin and scatter over the red onion. Drizzle with olive oil and salt and pepper and roast for 10 minutes.

2 Add the rice, wine, stock, rosemary and some salt and pepper and return to the oven for 20 minutes until the rice is almost tender and the liquid has almost all been absorbed. Scatter the mussels over the top of the rice. Cover tightly with foil and return to the oven for 15 minutes.

3 Remove the roasting tin from the oven, lift the foil and check the mussels, discarding any that haven't opened. Scatter over the chopped parsley. Serve at the table immediately, allowing guests to help themselves.

Oven-baked mussel and cherry tomato risotto

Tandoori-tikka king prawns

This isn't a classic Indian dish, it's one that I've brought together in the style of my favourite tandoori and tikka dry-cooked dishes. Serve it with a dollop of raita (or even tzatsiki) and a pile of chapatis, which you can now buy in supermarkets.

PREPARATION: 10 minutes COOKING TIME: 5 minutes

SERVES 4

1 garlic clove, crushed

1 teaspoon ground cumin

½ teaspoon chilli powder

½ teaspoon ground turmeric

½ teaspoon salt

150 g carton natural yoghurt

few drops of red food colouring (optional)

20 large raw, tiger prawns, shelled but tail section left intact

1 lemon, cut into wedges, chapatis and raita, to serve

METHOD

1 In a large, shallow dish, mix together the garlic, cumin, chilli, turmeric, salt, yoghurt and food colouring. Add the prawns and stir well to coat.

2 Pre-heat the grill to high, or heat a large, non-stick frying pan. Thread the prawns on to soaked bamboo skewers and cook for 5 minutes, turning until the coating is dark red and the prawns are cooked through. Serve with lemon wedges, raita and chapatis.

CHEF'S TIP: To make a quick raita, mix together a carton of natural yoghurt with some grated or diced cucumber, a crushed garlic clove, pinch of salt and sugar and some chopped fresh mint.

Tandoori-tikka king prawns

Crispy lemon fusion chicken

This may seem rather strange at first, cooking the floured chicken without any added fat, but providing you cook it good and slowly, the skin will gradually release enough fat to prevent any burning. The wine and stock are nicely thickened up by the cornflour, making a delicious France-meets-China fusion dish that you could serve French-style with puréed potatoes and green beans, or Chinese-style with boiled rice, pak choi and a splash of soy sauce.

PREPARATION: 15 minutes COOKING TIME: 30 minutes

SERVES 4

2 garlic cloves, finely chopped

grated rind and juice of 1 lemon

2 teaspoons Dijon mustard

1 teaspoon fresh thyme leaves plus 4 sprigs

8 boneless chicken thighs with skin on

3 tablespoons cornflour

100 ml (4½ fl oz) white wine

100 ml (4½ fl oz) chicken stock

salt and freshly ground black pepper

METHOD

1 Mix together the garlic, lemon rind, mustard, thyme leaves and some salt and pepper. Season the chicken thighs, then pull the skin back from the flesh. Spread with the mustard mixture, then stretch the skin back into place.

2 Season the cornflour with salt and pepper then roll the chicken thighs in the mixture. Set a large non-stick frying-pan over a low heat and, when hot, add the chicken thighs, skin-side down. Cook for 20 minutes without turning until the skin is crunchy and deep golden and the chicken is almost completely cooked through.

3 Turn over the chicken, pouring off any excess fat. Pour in the wine and lemon juice and add the thyme sprigs, then raise the heat and bubble rapidly for 3–4 minutes. Add the stock and simmer for a further 2–3 minutes until the sauce is smooth and thickened and the chicken is cooked through. Serve warm.

Oriental steamed
soy chicken and vegetables

For a really delicious low-fat meal that's healthy and easy to make, make a date with my Oriental Steamed Soy Chicken – you'll be hooked. To make this recipe you will need a large, two-tiered Oriental bamboo steamer.

PREPARATION: 10 minutes COOKING TIME: 15 minutes

SERVES 2

4 tablespoon soy sauce

1 tablespoon honey

pinch chilli flakes

2 chicken breasts or 4 chicken thighs, skinned, boned and cut into strips

100 g (4 oz) choi sum or pak choi

75 g (3 oz) shiitake mushrooms

50 g (2 oz) bean sprouts

2 salad onions, thinly sliced

boiled rice, to serve

METHOD

1 Mix the soy sauce, honey and chilli together in a shallow bowl. Add the chicken pieces, then place in a bamboo steamer. Cover and sit over a pan of boiling water for 10 minutes.

2 Cut the choi sum into 12 cm (4¾ inch) lengths or quarter the pak choi, and halve the mushrooms. Toss together and place in a second layer of the bamboo steamer. Scatter the bean sprouts and salad onions over the top.

3 Lift the steamer containing the chicken off the top of the pan and sit the vegetable tier underneath – it is crucial that the vegetables sit beneath the chicken otherwise the juices they release will all fall into the bowl holding the chicken and dilute the soy dressing.

4 Return the bamboo stack to the pan and continue to steam for a further 3–4 minutes until the vegetables are tender but still crisp and the chicken is cooked through.

5 Serve the bamboo steamer stack at the table with the rice, and allow guests to help themselves.

Mediterranean chicken caesar
with aïoli and foccacia croutons

This dish takes you on a Mediterranean tour with Italian croutons, Spanish dressing and Greek-style marinated chicken. Eat it in your back garden on a sunny afternoon and it'll be easy to imagine yourself in a Provençal olive grove.

PREPARATION: 20 minutes + marinating time   COOKING TIME: 20 minutes

SERVES 4

4 skinless, boneless chicken breasts

1 tablespoon chopped fresh rosemary

1 teaspoon dried oregano

1 shallot, finely chopped

100 ml (3 fl oz) red or white wine

2 tablespoons olive oil

salt and freshly ground black pepper

1 cos lettuce

FOR THE AÏOLI

4 tablespoons mayonnaise

1 crushed garlic clove

squeeze of fresh lemon juice

FOR THE CROUTONS

2 mini foccacia, or half a medium loaf, about 150 g (5 oz)

1 tablespoon olive oil

2 tablespoons freshly grated Parmesan

METHOD

1 Place the chicken breasts, rosemary, oregano, shallot, wine and olive oil in a shallow dish. Season with salt and pepper and set aside to marinate for at least 1 hour, but preferably overnight. Meanwhile, for the aïoli, mix the mayonnaise with the garlic then squeeze in a little lemon juice to taste.

2 Pre-heat the oven to 200°C/400°F/Gas 6. Remove the chicken from the marinade and place on a baking sheet. Roast for 20 minutes until golden brown and cooked through.

3 Meanwhile, make the croutons: cut the foccacia into cubes and toss with the olive oil and Parmesan. Scatter on to a baking sheet, ensuring they are in a single layer. Bake with the chicken for 5–10 minutes until crisp and golden brown, then remove from the oven and allow to cool.

4 Remove the chicken from the oven and allow to cool slightly, then cut diagonally into strips. Tear the cos lettuce into bite-sized pieces and place in a large salad bowl. Toss with the chicken strips, aïoli and croutons and serve while the chicken is still warm.

Mediterranean chicken caesar with aïoli and foccacia croutons

Chicken, sage and Cheddar
en croûte

Delicious straight from the oven or cooled and packed into a lunch box or picnic basket with a simple green salad. If you are serving these hot, try pairing them with my fiery Cracked Tapas Patatas Bravas on page 296.

PREPARATION: 15 minutes COOKING TIME: 25 minutes

SERVES 4

375 g pack ready-rolled puff pastry

4 small, skinless, boneless chicken breasts, each about 75 g (3 oz)

1 tablespoon Dijon mustard

8 fresh sage leaves

150 g (5 oz) coarsely grated Cheddar

1 tablespoon milk

salt and freshly ground black pepper

METHOD

1 Pre-heat the oven to 200°C/400°F/Gas 6. Open out the pastry on to a lightly floured board and roll out slightly so it is large enough to cut into four 15 x 20 cm (6 x 8 inch) rectangles. Spread the centre of each rectangle with the mustard and place a chicken fillet on each. Season with salt and pepper then place 2 sage leaves on each fillet.

2 Scatter the cheese evenly over each fillet, then dampen the edges of the pastry with a little water. Fold the pastry over to enclose the filling, squeezing together the edges between finger and thumb to ensure no melted cheese can escape during baking.

3 Transfer the parcels to a baking sheet, seam side down, then brush each with a little milk. Bake for 25 minutes until the pastry is crisp and deep golden and the chicken has cooked through. Serve hot or cold.

CHEF'S TIP: If you want to decorate your parcels, use a small, sharp knife to score a sage-shaped leaf on top of each before brushing with milk and baking. Alternatively, if you have any pastry trimmings left over, re-roll them, cut out leaf shapes and stick one to the surface of each parcel with a little water before baking.

Madras coconut, chicken
and banana curry

Moist, tender pieces of chicken in a rich almond, coconut and banana sauce – always a dinner winner in my house.

PREPARATION: 15 minutes COOKING TIME: 30 minutes

SERVES 4

1 teaspoon garam masala

1 tablespoon vegetable oil

8 skinless, boneless chicken thighs, halved

1 large onion, thinly sliced

2 tomatoes, roughly chopped

450 ml (¾ pint) chicken stock

2 tablespoons hot curry paste

142 ml carton double cream

50 g (2 oz) ground almonds

25 g (1 oz) desiccated coconut

2 large bananas

boiled rice, to serve

2 tablespoons roughly chopped fresh coriander

1 lemon cut into wedges, to garnish

METHOD

1 Mix together the chicken pieces, garam masala and some salt and pepper. Heat the oil in a large pan and add the chicken and onion and cook for 10 minutes, stirring occasionally until golden brown.

2 Add the tomatoes and cook for 2 minutes until beginning to soften. Pour in the stock, stir in the curry paste, then bring to the boil and simmer for 10 minutes.

3 Stir in the cream, almonds and the coconut. Peel the bananas and cut into 2 cm (¾ inch) thick slices. Add to the pan, season with salt and pepper to taste and simmer for 5 minutes until the bananas are just tender.

4 Divide between 4 plates and serve each with boiled rice, a sprinkling of fresh coriander and a wedge of lemon for squeezing over.

Coriander and lime chicken

I'm always looking for new ways of serving chicken, especially ones that are quick to make and really tasty. This dish is a real winner. I like to serve it with jasmine rice, steamed greens and a spicy dipping sauce (see Crispy Noodle-wrapped Prawns with Rice-wine Dipping Sauce, page 206). Leftovers are great served up the next day with a salad or in a French-bread sandwich.

PREPARATION: 15 minutes + marinating time   COOKING TIME: 15 minutes

SERVES 4

6 garlic cloves

4 tablespoons fresh coriander leaves, plus extra, to garnish

2 teaspoons black peppercorns, coarsely ground

2 teaspoons caster sugar

juice of 2 limes

2 teaspoons Thai fish sauce (nam pla)

1 tablespoon light soy sauce

1 tablespoon sunflower oil

4 skinless, boneless chicken breasts

METHOD

1   Finely chop the garlic and coriander then mix in the peppercorns, sugar, lime juice, fish sauce, soy sauce and sunflower oil until well blended. Place the chicken breasts in the marinade and set aside for 1–2 hours, turning from time to time.

2   Pre-heat a ridged griddle pan or heavy, non-stick frying-pan and cook the chicken for 7–8 minutes on each side until the chicken is cooked through and golden brown with good bar-marks. Serve hot or cold, garnished with coriander leaves.

CHEF'S TIP: The marinade contains lime juice, which tenderizes the chicken. After more than a few hours though, the meat fibres can become so soft that the chicken literally falls apart, which means that this dish is not suitable for overnight marinating.

Coriander and lime chicken *with* Simple wok noodles (page 305)

Superb lemon herb chicken
with roast potatoes

I know everyone thinks they know how to roast a chicken, but as this is the best recipe for a roast chicken in the whole world, I thought I'd share it with you. I have a chicken brick that I often cook this in, as it comes out moist and juicy with a miraculously crisp skin. If you don't own one (they cost around £10 from cook shops), cook it in the oven as detailed here. And don't save roast chicken and potatoes for Sundays, it's ideal for a casual after-work dinner party.

PREPARATION: 20 minutes COOKING TIME: 1½ hours

SERVES 4

1 medium chicken, about 1.5 kg (3¼ lb)

1 large lemon

large sprig of sage

large sprig of rosemary

25 g (1 oz) butter, at room temperature

2 garlic cloves, crushed

1 tablespoon olive oil

750 g (1½ lb) floury potatoes, such as King Edward or Maris Piper

sea salt and freshly ground black pepper

METHOD

1 Pre-heat the oven to 200°C/400°F/Gas 6. Snip any strings that are binding the chicken legs, then wipe inside the cavity with kitchen paper and season. Cut the lemon into 5 or 6 pieces and push them into the cavity with the sage and rosemary sprigs.

2 Mix together the butter and garlic with some salt and pepper. Loosen the skin on the breast then, using your fingers, spread the butter between the flesh and the skin. Pull the skin back into place. Place the bird in a large roasting tin and brush all over with a little oil and a sprinkling of coarse salt. Roast for 30 minutes.

3 Meanwhile, peel and cube the potatoes then cook in a pan of boiling water for exactly 5 minutes. Drain in a colander then shake vigorously to 'fluff up' the outside of the potatoes – this helps give them a lovely, crunchy finish when they are roasted.

4 Open the oven and quickly toss the potatoes into the pan, shaking to coat them in the buttery chicken juices. Return to the oven for 1 hour, without turning or poking until the chicken is cooked through and golden and the potatoes are crunchy and golden on the outside and fluffy and floury on the inside. Cut the chicken into quarters and serve with the pan juices and roasties.

Jamaican jerk chicken

I like to use chicken on the bone for my jerk chicken and find if I ask the butcher to cut a whole chicken into quarters, everyone gets to choose the piece they like best. Me, I'm a breast man.

PREPARATION: 20 minutes + marinating time COOKING TIME: 45 minutes

SERVES 4

2 onions, about 200 g (7 oz), roughly chopped

2 Scotch bonnet chillies, seeded and roughly chopped

2 garlic cloves

4 cm (1½ inch) piece root ginger, roughly chopped

2 teaspoons fresh marjoram leaves or fresh thyme

½ teaspoon ground allspice

120 ml (4 fl oz) cider vinegar

120 ml (4 fl oz) soy sauce

1 tablespoon honey

1.5 kg (3¼ lb) chicken (medium), quartered or 4 chicken quarters

salt and freshly ground black pepper

METHOD

1 Place the onions, chillies, garlic, ginger and marjoram in a food processor and blitz until well blended. Add the allspice, cider vinegar, soy sauce and honey and whizz again until smooth. Add salt and pepper to taste.

2 Deeply slash the chicken then place in a large, shallow dish. Pour over the sauce and chill for 2–3 hours, or overnight.

3 Pre-heat the oven to 200°C/400°F/Gas 6. Transfer the chicken to a rack and sit it inside a roasting tin. Pour over the marinade and roast for 40–45 minutes, basting occasionally with the marinating juices in the roasting tin until cooked through and blackened.

CHEF'S TIP: Jerk Chicken is delicious served with Peppy's Rice and Peas (see page 295).

This dish is also great cooked over medium-hot coals on the barbecue for 25–30 minutes. You'll need to baste it with the marinade and turn it occasionally to make sure it is thoroughly cooked.

Tender turkey and peanut butter curry

Normally seen at Christmas or Thanksgiving, turkey is an amazingly versatile, healthy and good-value food and deserves to be eaten all-year round. Here's a quick, one-pot recipe to whet your appetite.

PREPARATION: 15 minutes COOKING TIME: 45 minutes

SERVES 4

2 tablespoons vegetable oil

500 g (1 lb 2 oz) turkey escalopes or breast fillets, cubed

1 onion, chopped

2 garlic cloves, chopped

2 green chillies, seeded and chopped

2 teaspoons chopped fresh ginger

2 tablespoons Madras curry powder

400 g can chopped tomatoes

200 ml carton coconut cream

2 tablespoons crunchy peanut butter

2 tablespoons chopped fresh coriander

salt and freshly ground black pepper

pilau rice, to serve

METHOD

1 Pre-heat the oven to 190°C/375°F/Gas 5. Heat the oil in a casserole dish and stir-fry the turkey, onion, garlic, chillies, ginger and curry powder for 5 minutes until beginning to brown.

2 Add some salt and pepper then stir in the tomatoes, coconut cream and peanut butter. Cover with a tightly fitting lid and bake for 45 minutes. Check the seasoning, stir in the coriander and serve with pilau rice.

Cinnamon-scented duck
on cherry sauce

Call me old-fashioned if you like, but this is a classic and I want to see it back on our tables. You don't need to add any oil to the pan when frying the duck as the natural fat will be released as it cooks. Serve with Rösti Dauphinoise (page 294).

PREPARATION: 15 minutes + 1 hour marinating time COOKING TIME: 15 minutes

SERVES 4

4 x 225 g (8 oz) skin-on duck breasts

½ teaspoon sea salt

½ teaspoon ground cinnamon

100 ml (4 fl oz) ruby port

425 g can pitted black cherries in syrup

4 fresh thyme sprigs, plus extra for garnish, if liked

½ teaspoon balsamic vinegar

METHOD

1 Prick the skin on the duck breasts with a fork, then rub in the salt and cinnamon. Place the port, the juice from the cherries and the thyme in a shallow dish and sit the duck skin-side up in the mixture so the flesh marinates while the skin takes in the salt and cinnamon. Set aside for 1 hour.

2 Pat the duck dry. Heat a large, non-stick frying-pan and cook the duck, skin-side down for 8–10 minutes until crisp and golden. Remove the duck from the pan and drain off all the excess fat.

3 Return the duck to the pan skin-side up. Pour round the marinade mixture, bring to the boil and simmer for 12–15 minutes until the duck is cooked through but still a little pink in the centre. Remove the duck from the pan and rest on a plate for a few minutes.

4 Check the seasoning and stir in the cherries and balsamic vinegar. Simmer for a minute or two until the cherries are warmed through. Then, spoon the cherry sauce onto the plates, place the breasts on top of the sauce and garnish with a sprig of fresh thyme, if liked.

Cinnamon-scented duck on cherry sauce *with* Rösti dauphinoise (page 294)

Warm Oriental duck
and mango salad

It's essential that food looks good as well as tasting terrific – and this salad looks and tastes fabulous. It's also low in fat and quick to prepare – the perfect Oriental nosh.

PREPARATION: 15 minutes COOKING TIME: 5 minutes

SERVES 4

450 g (1 lb) skinless, boneless duck breasts

1 teaspoon Chinese five spice

1 teaspoon sunflower oil

FOR THE DRESSING

juice of 1 lime

1 teaspoon Thai fish sauce (nam pla)

1 tablespoon soy sauce

2 teaspoons clear honey

FOR THE SALAD

80 g bag mixed baby leaves

1 small mango, skinned, stoned and cut into matchsticks

100 g (4 oz) bean sprouts

4 salad onions, shredded

fresh mint leaves and toasted sesame seeds, to garnish

METHOD

1 Cut the duck into 1 cm (¾ inch) wide strips and mix with the five spice. Heat the oil in a wok or large frying-pan and, when hot, add the duck strips and stir-fry for exactly 2 minutes until nicely browned but still a little pink in the centre.

2 Transfer to a large bowl and stir in the lime juice, fish sauce, soy sauce and clear honey. Set aside to cool to room temperature.

3 To serve, place the salad leaves in a large serving bowl and toss with the mango, bean sprouts and duck with dressing. Scatter over the shredded salad onions, mint and sesame seeds and serve.

CHEF'S TIP: This is a very pretty dish, but for added attraction, place the shredded salad onions in a bowl of iced water so they curl.

Lasagnette
with smoked ham and minted peas

This is one of those great pasta recipes that are ready to serve in the time it takes the pasta to cook. If you fancy it, stir in a slosh of double cream just before serving.

PREPARATION: 5 minutes COOKING TIME: 10 minutes

SERVES 4

300 g (11 oz) dried lasagnette or other pasta ribbons

2 tablespoons olive oil

1 small onion, finely chopped

200 g (7 oz) thick-cut smoked ham

150 g (5 oz) frozen peas, thawed

splash of white wine, stock or water, about 4 tablespoons

2 tablespoons chopped fresh mint

salt and freshly ground black pepper

freshly grated Parmesan, to serve

METHOD

1 Cook the pasta in a large pan of boiling, salted water, according to the packet instructions.

2 Meanwhile, heat the oil in a frying-pan and cook the onion for 3–4 minutes until beginning to soften.

3 Cut the smoked ham into strips about 5 mm (¼ inch) wide and 3 cm (1¼ inches) long. Add to the pan and cook for 1 minute then add the peas and liquid and simmer for 4–5 minutes until the liquid has evaporated. Season to taste with a little salt and plenty of black pepper.

4 Drain the pasta and return to the pan. Add the pea mixture and the mint and toss well together. Divide between bowls and pass round the Parmesan.

Crusted roast rump steak
with crispy speckled onion rings

This is my ideal Saturday supper – roasted rump steak with a caper, tomato and basil crust, lots of crispy onion rings – and it takes minimum time to prepare. Serve with a robust red wine and a crisp green salad.

PREPARATION: 20 minutes COOKING TIME: 25 minutes

SERVES 4

1 Spanish onion

300 ml (½ pint) milk

vegetable oil, for frying

6 tablespoons self-raising flour

2 teaspoons snipped chives

salt and freshly ground black pepper

FOR THE STEAKS

4 x 150 g (5 oz) steaks

1 slice of white bread, about 50 g (2 oz)

12 capers

4 sun-dried tomatoes in oil, roughly chopped

1 ripe tomato, roughly chopped

1 tablespoon of olive oil, or oil from the sun-dried tomato jar

handful of fresh basil, roughly chopped

METHOD

1 Begin by putting the onion rings in to soak for a minimum of 15 minutes. Cut the onion into 1 cm (½ inch) wide slices and separate the rings. Pour over the milk and set aside, turning the onion rings occasionally. Take the steaks out of the fridge and leave at room temperature for 20 minutes or so.

2 Pre-heat the oven to 220°C/425°F/Gas 7. Break the bread into pieces and whizz in a food processor to form rough crumbs. Remove and set aside. Then, place the capers, sun-dried and fresh tomatoes, the oil, basil and some salt and pepper in the food processor and whizz until pulped. Add the breadcrumbs and pulse once more until evenly mixed.

3 Place the steaks on a lightly oiled baking sheet and spoon over the tomato-crumb mixture. Cook in the oven for 10 minutes until the steaks are browned but still a little pink in the centre. Meanwhile, heat 5 cm (2 inches) of oil in a deep frying pan. Mix together the flour, chives and some salt and pepper. Drain the onion rings, dust in the flour, shaking off any excess, then fry in batches for 2–3 minutes until crisp and golden brown. Drain on kitchen paper.

4 Transfer the steaks to 4 warm serving plates and allow to rest for a few minutes. Pile the speckled onion rings on the side, garnish with fresh basil leaves and serve.

Crusted roast rump steak with crispy speckled onion rings

One-pot chunky
beef bourguignonne

This is a classic that never fails to go down well. And while you've got the oven on, why not pop in some Rösti Dauphinoise (page 294). It's an ideal accompaniment, as is my scrumptious Soft, Bellissima Dolcelatte Polenta (page 290). Ooh, so exciting, and all in one pot, too.

PREPARATION: 20 minutes   COOKING TIME: 2 hours

SERVES 6

2 tablespoons olive oil

750 g (1½ lb) cubed braising or stewing steak

3 tablespoons flour, seasoned with salt and pepper

9 shallots, halved

3 garlic cloves, halved

125 g (4½ oz) lardons or cubed pancetta

75 cl bottle red wine

2 sprigs fresh thyme

1 tablespoon tomato purée

250 g (9 oz) button mushrooms

salt and freshly ground black pepper

METHOD

1 Pre-heat the oven to 180°C/350°F/Gas 4. Set a 3 litre (5½ pint) flameproof casserole with a lid over the heat and add the olive oil.

2 Toss the meat in the seasoned flour then cook in batches in the hot oil for 3–4 minutes until nicely browned. Remove each batch with a slotted spoon and set aside. Now cook the shallots, garlic and pancetta in the pan for 5 minutes, stirring frequently until golden brown.

3 Return the meat to the pan then pour in the wine and bring to a steaming boil. Stir in the thyme, tomato purée and some seasoning. Cover with the lid and cook in the oven for 1 hour. Add the mushrooms, cover and return to the oven for a further 30–45 minutes until the meat is tender. Serve straight from the casserole.

One-pot chunky beef bourguignonne *with* Soft, bellissima, Dolcelatte polenta (page 290)

Spicy Thai beef salad

A delicious, hot, sweet-and-sour salad which is typical of north-east Thailand. It also traditionally includes some ground rice, which I like, but can be skipped if you're short on time. I serve it with some sticky Thai rice for a lovely supper or dinner-party main course.

PREPARATION: 25 minutes COOKING TIME: 1 minute

SERVES 4

4 tablespoons long-grain rice

juice of 2 limes

4 tablespoons Thai fish sauce (nam pla)

1 tablespoon caster sugar

½ teaspoon chilli powder

2 shallots, very thinly sliced

2 garlic cloves, finely chopped

2 tablespoons chopped fresh mint leaves

1 Thai red chilli, thinly sliced

1 tablespoon vegetable oil

450 g (1 lb) tender steak, such as sirloin or fillet, cut into fine 1 x 3 cm (½ x 1¼ inch) strips

FOR THE SALAD

1 heart of cos lettuce, roughly torn

150 g (5 oz) bean sprouts

150 g (5 oz) fine green beans, blanched and cooled

METHOD

1 Heat a large, non-stick frying pan and cook the rice for a couple of minutes, stirring until the grains start to turn golden and begin to pop. Transfer to a pestle and mortar and grind to a coarse powder.

2 Arrange the salad on 4 serving plates.

3 In a large bowl, stir together the lime juice, fish sauce, caster sugar and chilli powder, mixing until well blended. Stir in the shallots, garlic, mint, fresh chilli and ground rice.

4 Heat the oil in the pan and, when very hot, add the beef and stir-fry for exactly 30 seconds until browned on the outside but still pink in the centre. Stir into the dressing bowl then, while still slightly warm, spoon over the salad. Serve immediately.

CHEF'S TIP: This can be made in advance; just stir-fry the steak at the last minute and spoon over the salad.

Spicy Thai beef salad

Lamb, mint and chilli strudels

This is the most brilliant way to use left-over lamb. I tend to shred whatever's left on the Sunday lamb joint and turn it into these delicious strudels which, when paired with a salad such as my Fennel, Orange and Olive Salad (page 304) make a lovely, light supper. Like my Chicken, Sage and Cheddar en Croûte (page 240), these are perfect for picnics or packed lunches.

PREPARATION: 15 minutes   COOKING TIME: 15 minutes

SERVES 4

300 g (11 oz) cooked lamb, shredded

2 tablespoons mint jelly

1 teaspoon West Indian hot pepper sauce or good dash of Tabasco

salt and freshly ground black pepper

4 sheets filo pastry

knob of butter, melted

METHOD

1 Pre-heat the oven to 220°C/425°F/Gas 7. Mix together the lamb, mint jelly and pepper sauce. Add salt and pepper to taste.

2 Open out a sheet of filo pastry and scatter over one quarter of the mixture. Fold 1 cm (½ inch) of the edges on the longer side of the pastry over the filling, then roll up like a swiss roll. Arrange seam side down on a non-stick baking sheet.

3 Repeat to make 4 rolls. Brush with melted butter and bake for 12–15 minutes until crisp and golden brown.

Lightning lamb cassoulet

A classic French cassoulet takes ages to prepare and cook. My simplified version is tasty, easy and pretty quick to get together. It's hearty, so make sure your guests are good and hungry.

PREPARATION: 10 minutes COOKING TIME: 1 hour 15 minutes

SERVES 4

1 tablespoon olive oil

8 lamb cutlets

1 small onion, finely chopped

2 garlic cloves, finely chopped

400 g can chopped tomatoes

1 teaspoon dried herbes de Provence

1 teaspoon brown sugar

1 tablespoon red wine vinegar

150 ml (¼ pint) lamb stock

2 x 400 g can cannellini beans, drained

75 g (3 oz) fresh white breadcrumbs

salt and freshly ground white pepper

METHOD

1 Pre-heat the oven to 180°C/350°F/Gas 4. Heat the oil in a large frying-pan and quickly brown the lamb cutlets for 2 minutes on each side. Remove from the pan and transfer to a 2 litre (3½ pint) casserole dish.

2 Add the onion and garlic to the pan and cook for 3–4 minutes until softened and golden. Add the tomatoes, herbs, sugar, vinegar and lamb stock and simmer together for 2–3 minutes. Add salt and pepper to taste.

3 Empty the beans over the lamb cutlets then roughly stir in the tomato mixture. Sprinkle the breadcrumbs on top of the casserole in an even layer, cover and bake for 30 minutes. Remove the cover and cook for a further 30 minutes until bubbling and golden brown on top.

Lamb shank Rogan Josh

Rogan Josh is one of those classic Indian dishes which has many interpretations. This is my version and it's lovely. I like to use meat on the bone such as lamb shanks, as the bones add flavour to the dish while the lamb slow-cooks until meltingly tender. Pair it with my Easy Pilau Rice (page 300) for a delicious supper.

PREPARATION: 25 minutes COOKING TIME: 2½–3 hours

SERVES 4

2 tablespoons plain flour

1 tablespoon chilli powder

1 teaspoon ground coriander

½ teaspoon ground ginger

½ teaspoon salt

pinch of nutmeg

4 lamb shanks, each about 500 g (1 lb 2 oz)

2 tablespoons vegetable oil

1 large onion, thinly sliced

300 ml (½ pint) Greek-style natural yoghurt

450 ml (¾ pint) hot lamb stock

4 cardamom pods, cracked

1 pinch saffron strands

4 small tomatoes, each cut into 6 wedges

METHOD

1 Mix together the flour, chilli powder, coriander, ginger, salt and nutmeg. Dust the lamb shanks in the flour, reserving any excess.

2 Pre-heat the oven to 180°C/350°F/Gas 4. Pour the oil into a large roasting tin and place over a high heat. Cook the lamb shanks for 10 minutes, turning until well browned, then transfer to a large plate and set aside.

3 Add the onion to the pan and cook for 10 minutes until golden brown. Add the reserved spiced flour and cook for 1 minute, stirring continuously. Stir in the yoghurt and stock.

4 Return the lamb to the pan. Add the cardamom and saffron and bring to the boil. Cover tightly with foil and cook for 1½ hours. Add the tomato wedges and cook for a further 40–60 minutes until the lamb is almost falling away from the bone. Serve hot.

CHEF'S TIP: The longer this is cooked, the more tender the lamb becomes. It can cook for up to 3 hours, but remember to keep it tightly covered and add a splash of water or stock if it starts to dry out.

Lamb shank Rogan Josh *with* Easy pilau rice (page 300) *and* Ceylonese spiced runner beans (page 298)

Ainsley's special red-wine spaghetti bolognese

You all know how to make bolognese – it's a real favourite with us Brits – but mine does have a great twist. I marinate it overnight in wine so it's really succulent and very tender. Go on, try it. You'll be glad you did.

PREPARATION: 20 minutes + overnight marinating COOKING TIME: 1 hour 5 minutes

SERVES 4-6

250 g (9 oz) minced beef

250 g (9 oz) minced lamb

75 cl bottle Italian red wine, such as Chianti

½ teaspoon dried oregano

1 tablespoon olive oil

1 onion, finely chopped

2 garlic cloves, finely chopped

400 g can chopped tomatoes

pinch dried chilli flakes

1 tablespoon tomato purée

450 g (1 lb) dried spaghetti

3 tablespoons chopped fresh parsley

salt and freshly ground black pepper

freshly grated Parmesan, to serve

METHOD

1 Place all the minced meat in a bowl and stir in the red wine, oregano and some salt and pepper. Cover with cling film and chill for at least 4 hours or up to 12.

2 Heat the oil in a large pan and cook the onion and garlic for 3–4 minutes until softened and golden. Add the mince and any wine left in the bottom of the bowl with the tomatoes, chilli, purée and some salt and pepper. Bring to the boil then cover and simmer for 45 minutes. Remove the lid and bubble fairly rapidly for 15 minutes until you have a rich, dark sauce.

3 Cook the spaghetti in a large pan of boiling, salted water until tender. Drain well and return to the pan.

4 Stir the parsley through the sauce and check the seasoning. Add to the pan of spaghetti and mix through. Divide between bowls and serve with freshly grated Parmesan and a few glasses of Chianti.

Ainsley's special red-wine spaghetti bolognese

Crunchy rösti-coated lamb patties

These are tasty Greek-style burgers with a difference – a crunchy potato coating that adds real bite and style to the finished dish. There is a picture of this recipe on page 297.

PREPARATION: 20 minutes COOKING TIME: 20 minutes

SERVES 4

1 shallot, roughly chopped

2 garlic cloves, roughly chopped

2 tablespoons chopped fresh mint

500 g (1 lb 2 oz) minced lamb

½ teaspoon dried rosemary

200 g (7 oz) feta, roughly chopped

2 tablespoons flour, seasoned with salt and pepper

1 large egg, beaten with 1 tablespoon cold water

1 large floury potato, such as King Edward, about 200 g (7 oz)

vegetable oil, for shallow-frying

salt and freshly ground black pepper

METHOD

1 Place the shallot, garlic and mint in the food processor and whizz until finely chopped. Add the lamb, rosemary and some salt and pepper and whizz again until the mince is fine and well mixed. Add the feta and pulse 2–3 times until the feta is roughly mixed into the mince but isn't finely chopped.

2 Shape the mixture into 8 even-sized cakes. Dust the cakes in seasoned flour then roll in the beaten egg.

3 Coarsely grate the potato on to a large plate, then roll the patties until lightly coated in potato.

4 Heat 1 cm (½ in) of oil in a large, non-stick frying-pan and cook the patties in batches for 5 minutes on each side until crisp, golden brown and cooked through, though still a little pink in the centre. Serve hot.

CHEF'S TIP: I like to serve these with a spoonful of tomato chutney or relish. And why not try them with one of the fresh tomato salsas that many supermarkets now stock?

Greek-style lamb parcels
en papillote

Succulent lamb steak cooked in onion, garlic and herbs in its own steamed parcel. Try serving with Mama's Greek Butter-bean Salad (page 284).

PREPARATION: 10 minutes COOKING TIME: 30 minutes

SERVES 4

4 x 250 g (9 oz) lamb leg steaks (bone in)

1 tablespoon olive oil

1 small red onion, thinly sliced

2 garlic cloves, finely chopped

1 teaspoon dried oregano

4 fresh bay leaves

100 ml (3½ fl oz) white wine

1 teaspoon cracked black pepper

sea salt

METHOD

1 Pre-heat the oven to 200°C/400°F/Gas 6.

2 Cut four 40 cm (16 inch) circles out of baking parchment. Rub each circle with a little olive oil, then place a leg steak on one half. Scatter over the onion, garlic, oregano, and a little salt and pepper.

3 Top with a bay leaf then fold in half to form a semi-circle. Fold over the edges to seal then, just before you have completely enclosed the steak, pour in a little wine, then finish off the folding, ensuring that the steaks are completely sealed.

4 Place the parcels on a baking sheet and bake for 30 minutes. Carefully transfer each parcel to a plate and serve.

CHEF'S TIP: To make a circle out of a square of baking parchment, fold it in half along the diagonal, then fold again. Continue folding until the paper forms an arrow-head shape. Cut the opposite end to the point of the arrow into a round. When you open the paper out you should have a circle.

Braised bacon vin blanc

A nicely cured bacon joint is a wonderful thing, especially when braised in a tasty stock like this one here. I like to serve it with my Sweet-potato and Coriander Mash (page 288). Left-overs will keep, wrapped in foil in the fridge, for quite a few days and make fantastic sandwiches and salads.

PREPARATION: 10 minutes + resting time COOKING TIME: 1½ hours

SERVES 6

1 kg (2¼ lb) bacon joint

300 ml (½ pint) dry white wine

300 ml (½ pint) vegetable stock

1 teaspoon peppercorns

2 star anise

1 onion, roughly chopped

1 apple, roughly chopped

METHOD

1 Pre-heat the oven to 180°C/350°F/Gas 4. Place the bacon in a roasting tin with the wine, stock, peppercorns, star anise, onion and apple. Cover tightly with foil and roast for 1 hour.

2 Remove the foil and cook for a further 30 minutes until the bacon is golden brown. Transfer the bacon to a warm plate and leave to rest for at least 15 minutes before carving. Serve warm or chilled.

CHEF'S TIP: For a delicious gravy, strain the stock into a pan and thicken with a teaspoon of dissolved cornflour. Add a tablespoonful of redcurrant jelly and a dash of balsamic vinegar, but don't add any salt.

Smoked bacon and Dolcelatte risotto

Oh, I love a good old risotto, me, and this one is a corker. It needs nothing more with it, except, maybe, a glass of fruity red wine.

PREPARATION: 10 minutes COOKING TIME: 30 minutes

SERVES 4

25 g (1 oz) butter

1 small onion, finely chopped

1 large garlic clove, finely chopped

200 g (7 oz) smoked streaky bacon, cut widthways into thin strips

300 g (11 oz) risotto rice, such as Arborio or Carnaroli

750 ml (¾ pint) hot chicken stock

2 tablespoons chopped fresh parsley

150 g (5 oz) dolcelatte

salt and freshly ground black pepper

METHOD

1 Heat the butter in a sauté pan and cook the onion, garlic and bacon for 5 minutes until softened and golden brown. Stir in the rice and cook for 1 minute.

2 Gradually stir in the stock, cooking for about 20 minutes until the grains are tender and all the liquid has been absorbed. Stir in the parsley and season with a tiny touch of salt (the cheese you're about to add is salty) and some black pepper.

3 Roughly dice the cheese and stir into the risotto. Quickly divide the risotto between 4 bowls, before the cheese has completely melted, and finish with a good grind of black pepper.

CHEF'S TIPS: Dolcelatte is delicious in this dish but a good alternative to look out for in your local cheese shop or supermarket is creamy Gorgonzola – avoid regular Gorgonzola, often labelled as Gorgonzola picante, as its flavour is a little too strong for this recipe.

If your risotto is a little too stodgy by the time you come to serve it, simply stir in a little more stock and a splash of cream before you take it to the table.

Pan-fried pork chops with
glazed apples, cider and cream sauce

We all know that pork and apples go together like love and marriage, and it couldn't be proved any better than in this lovely, up-to-the-minute classic. I like to serve it with a soft mash and some buttery greens.

PREPARATION: 10 minutes COOKING TIME: 25 minutes

SERVES 4

1 tablespoon vegetable oil

2 Cox's Orange Pippin apples, each cut into 8 wedges

4 x 200 g (7 oz) pork chops

2 sprigs fresh sage

200 ml (7 fl oz) dry cider

1 tablespoon redcurrant jelly

200 ml carton crème fraîche

salt and freshly ground black pepper

METHOD

1 Heat the oil in a large non-stick frying-pan and cook the apples for 3–4 minutes on each side until golden brown but still firm. Transfer to a plate and set aside.

2 Season the chops with salt and pepper and add to the pan. Cook for 5 minutes until golden brown, turning once. Add the sage and cider and simmer for 15 minutes until the chops are cooked through. Use a slotted spoon to transfer the pork to a large plate. Cover with foil and leave to rest for a few minutes.

3 Stir the redcurrant jelly into the pan and simmer for 2–3 minutes, stirring until the jelly dissolves. Stir in the crème fraîche and apples, heat through gently and season to taste.

4 Pour any juices from the pork into the pan, then divide the chops between 4 plates, spoon over the apples and sauce and serve with some green vegetables.

Pan-fried pork chops with glazed apples, cider and cream sauce

Herbed couscous wedges
with roast vine-tomatoes and rocket

Couscous makes a welcome change from other everyday grains such as rice. It can get a little sticky and I've used this characteristic to my advantage in this dish, where I add a little more liquid than usual and allow the couscous to set into a firm cake.

PREPARATION: 15 minutes COOKING TIME: 20 minutes

SERVES 4

pinch of saffron strands

1 crushed garlic clove

1 vegetable stock cube

300 ml (½ pint) boiling water

250 g (9 oz) couscous

2 tablespoons toasted pine nuts

3 tablespoons chopped fresh parsley

2 tablespoons olive oil

4 cherry tomato vines, each with 5–7 tomatoes

50 g packet wild rocket

1 lemon, cut into wedges

salt and freshly ground black pepper

METHOD

1 Pre-heat the oven to 200°C/400°F/Gas 6. Place the saffron, garlic and stock cube in a heatproof jug then pour over the boiling water, stirring until the cube dissolves.

2 Place the couscous in a heatproof bowl and pour over the stock mixture. Stir in the pine nuts and parsley and season to taste. Brush a 23 cm (9 inch) dinner plate with a little of the olive oil and spoon in the couscous mixture. Smooth the surface over with the back of a spoon then set aside to cool completely.

3 Place the tomatoes in a small roasting tin and drizzle with the remaining oil. Roast for 20 minutes until the tomatoes are tender and the skins have split.

4 Turn the couscous out on to a plate and cut into 4 wedges. Pile the rocket leaves on top of the couscous, then top each serving with a roasted vine of tomatoes. Drizzle over any pan juices and serve a lemon wedge on the side of each for squeezing over.

Cumin-curried chickpea
and spinach burgers

Chickpeas make a great veggie-burger base and they taste fantastic when spiced up with a little cumin seed and curry paste. If you're feeding kids, opt for a milder curry paste than the h-h-h-h-hot one I go for.

PREPARATION: 20 minutes COOKING TIME: 20 minutes

SERVES 6

1 tablespoon olive oil

1 small onion, finely chopped

2 teaspoons cumin seeds

225 g (8 oz) young spinach leaves

1 tablespoon hot curry paste

2 x 400 g cans chick peas, drained

2 tablespoons crunchy peanut butter

25 g (1 oz) fresh white breadcrumbs

salt and freshly ground black pepper

vegetable oil, for shallow-frying

burger buns or salad, to serve

METHOD

1 Heat the olive oil in a large frying pan and cook the onion for 2–3 minutes until beginning to soften. Add the cumin seeds, cook for 1 minute then add the spinach and cook over a high heat for 5 minutes until the spinach has wilted and any water released has evaporated. Stir in the curry paste and remove from the heat.

2 Place the chickpeas in a food processor with the peanut butter and breadcrumbs and whizz to form a thick paste. Add the spinach mixture and some seasoning and pulse until well blended. Using damp hands, shape the mixture into 6 even-sized cakes.

3 Wipe out the frying-pan with some kitchen paper and heat 1–2 tablespoons of the vegetable oil. Cook the burgers in batches for 4–5 minutes on each side until golden brown. Serve warm, sandwiched in a bread bun or with a stack of fresh salad.

Clare's winter-vegetable cobbler

This is just the kind of modernized classic that's reappearing in all those trendy pub-restaurants. It's also a perfect family supper – warming, very tasty and easy to make at home.

PREPARATION: 15 minutes COOKING TIME: 50 minutes

SERVES 6

2 leeks, thickly sliced

6 small carrots, cubed

6 small parsnips, cubed

4 sage sprigs

2 tablespoons olive oil

300 ml (½ pint) vegetable stock

142 ml carton double cream

1 tablespoon wholegrain mustard

salt and freshly ground black pepper

FOR THE COBBLES

175 g (6 oz) self-raising flour

½ teaspoon salt

¼ teaspoon cayenne

25 g (1 oz) butter

75 g (3 oz) mature Cheddar, finely grated

1 large egg

3 tablespoons milk

METHOD

1 Pre-heat the oven to 200°C/400°F/Gas 6. Place the vegetables and sage in a roasting tin, drizzle with oil and season with salt and pepper. Roast for 30 minutes until nicely browned.

2 Meanwhile, place the flour, salt, cayenne, butter and three quarters of the cheese in a food processor and whizz until well blended. Beat together the egg and 2 tablespoons of the milk then add to the food processor. Pulse to form a smooth, soft dough.

3 Mix together the stock, cream and mustard, and pour over the vegetables. Then, with floured hands, roll the cobble mixture into 6 balls and flatten slightly with the heel of the hand. Brush the tops of the cobbles with the remaining milk, then scatter over the reserved cheese.

4 Carefully place the cobbles on top of the vegetables and sauce and bake for 20 minutes until risen and golden brown. Serve immediately.

Artichoke and Gorgonzola
Pizza

This pizza is ready in next to no time and because of the choice of toppings it looks really quite sophisticated. I always keep a packet of pizza-base mix in the store-cupboard and there's often a wedge of blue cheese lurking in the back of my fridge, so I find it ideal for entertaining last-minute guests. I often serve my Roast Aubergine and Mint Salad (page 292) or my Fennel, Orange and Olive Salad (page 304) on the side.

PREPARATION: 15 minutes + 10 minutes rising time   COOKING TIME: 20 minutes

SERVES 4

2 x 145 g sachets pizza dough mix

250 ml (8 fl oz) warm water

285 g jar artichokes in olive oil, well drained

150 g (5 oz) Gorgonzola or dolcelatte

freshly ground black pepper

2 tablespoons snipped fresh chives, to garnish

METHOD

1 Pre-heat the oven to 220°C/425°F/Gas 7. Place two large baking sheets in the oven.

2 Empty the pizza dough mix into a large bowl, pour in the warm water, then bring together to make a soft dough. On a floured board, knead the dough vigorously for 5 minutes until smooth and stretchy.

3 Halve the dough and roll each piece into a 23 cm (9 inch) round. Place each circle on to a sheet of floured baking parchment. Arrange the artichokes evenly over each base, then crumble over the cheese; season with black pepper. Leave to rise for 10 minutes.

4 Remove the hot baking sheets from the oven and carefully slide a pizza on to each. Bake for 15–20 minutes until the base is golden and cooked through. Scatter over the chives and serve warm.

Caramelized-onion and red-pepper penne

A simple dish that's full of flavour and colour, and is so satisfying.

PREPARATION: 10 minutes   COOKING TIME: 45 minutes

SERVES 4

4 tablespoons olive oil

4 red peppers, seeded and cut lengthways into 1 cm wide strips

1 large onion, sliced

300 g (11 oz) dried penne or other pasta shapes

handful of fresh basil

salt and freshly ground black pepper

freshly grated Parmesan, to serve

METHOD

1   Heat the oil in a large, non-stick frying-pan and cook the peppers over a medium heat for 15 minutes. Add the onion and cook for a further 30 minutes until the peppers and onions are very soft and nicely browned. You will need to keep them on a fairly high heat so that the moisture from the vegetables evaporates. Stir from time to time so they don't catch on the bottom and burn and add a splash more oil if they start to stick. Add salt and pepper to taste.

2   Meanwhile, cook the pasta in a large pan of boiling water according to packet instructions. Drain the pasta well and return to the pan. Add the pepper mixture and the basil and mix well together.

3   Divide between 4 bowls and scatter with freshly grated Parmesan.

CHEF'S TIP: If you have any left-overs, transfer to a heatproof dish, top with a few cubes of mozzarella or grated Cheddar and bake at 200°C/400°F/Gas 6 for 15 minutes or so until piping hot.

Baked hedgehog tatties

My kids go mad for these Baked Hedgehog Tatties. They love the different colours of the herbs, tomatoes, courgettes and mozzarella and adore the taste. Wicked, Dad, wicked!

PREPARATION: 20 minutes COOKING TIME: 1 hour 25 minutes

SERVES 4

4 x 250 g (9 oz) baking potatoes

3 tablespoons olive oil

1 garlic clove, crushed

1 teaspoon chopped fresh rosemary

4 plum tomatoes, thinly sliced lengthways

4 baby courgettes, thinly sliced lengthways

150 g (5 oz) ball mozzarella, thinly sliced

salt and freshly ground black pepper

METHOD

1 Pre-heat the oven to 200°C/400°F/Gas 6. Scrub, dry and prick the potatoes with a fork. Place them directly on the oven shelf and cook for 1 hour.

2 Meanwhile, mix together the olive oil, garlic and rosemary and some salt and pepper.

3 With padded oven gloves, take the potatoes out of the oven. Make deep cuts widthways about 1 cm (½ inch) apart in each potato, taking care not to cut right through. Slot the tomatoes, courgettes and mozzarella into the slices, arranging and alternating them so they all fit evenly into the potatoes. If the potato starts to break up, don't worry, just thread a skewer through to keep everything together.

4 Transfer the hot potatoes to a baking sheet and drizzle over the rosemary oil. Bake for a further 20–25 minutes until the cheese is melted and bubbling and the vegetables are tinged with golden brown. Maddie, Jimmy, tea's ready. Come and get it!

Goats' cheese and beet leaf tortilla

I love the combination of tangy goats' cheese and the slightly bitter beet leaves. You can get beet leaves from your local greengrocer or look out for salad bags of them in the supermarket. Good alternatives include red chard and spinach. I like to serve this with my Cracked Tapas Patatas Bravas (page 296) or a simple salad.

PREPARATION: 15 minutes COOKING TIME: 10 minutes

SERVES 2

200 g (7 oz) young beet or spinach leaves

2 tablespoons olive oil

1 shallot, thinly sliced

1 garlic clove, thinly sliced

1 teaspoon chopped fresh rosemary

6 eggs

100 g (4 oz) firm, creamy goats' cheese

salt and freshly ground black pepper

METHOD

1 Bring a large pan of salted water to the boil and cook the beet leaves for just 30 seconds. Drain well and cool under cold water.

2 Heat 1 tablespoon of the oil in a 20 cm (8 inch) non-stick frying-pan and cook the shallot and garlic for 3–4 minutes until softened. Add the rosemary and cook for a further 30 seconds.

3 Meanwhile, in a large bowl, whisk together the eggs with some salt and pepper. Then stir through the cooled beet leaves and the onion mixture. Add the remaining oil to the hot pan, pour in the egg mixture and cook for 1 minute or so, stirring until the egg begins to set.

4 Crumble the goats' cheese over the top of the tortilla and continue to cook over a low heat for a further 5 minutes until the egg is almost completely set – take care not to burn the underneath.

5 Pre-heat the grill to medium. Place the pan under the grill for 2–3 minutes until golden brown and completely set. Slice and serve.

Mouth-watering mushroom and salad-onion risotto

Spend a little time next to your cooker for a truly creamy, cheesy, mouth-watering experience. Go on, it's worth it.

PREPARATION: 20 minutes COOKING TIME: 25 minutes

SERVES 4

10 g packet dried porcini mushrooms

300 ml (½ pint) boiling water

25 g (1 oz) butter

1 bunch salad onions, thinly sliced

2 garlic cloves, finely chopped

300 g (10 oz) mixed mushrooms, such as chestnut, morel and oyster, sliced

300 g (10 oz) risotto rice such as Arborio or Carnaroli

600 ml (1 pint) hot vegetable stock

142 ml carton double cream

50 g (2 oz) Parmesan, freshly grated

2 tablespoons chopped fresh parsley

salt and freshly ground black pepper

METHOD

1 Place the dried mushrooms in a heatproof bowl and cover with the boiling water. Set aside for 20 minutes.

2 Heat the butter in a large pan and add the salad onions, garlic and mushrooms with some salt and pepper and cook gently for 5 minutes until softened. Remove the mixture with a slotted spoon and set aside.

3 Add the rice to the buttery pan and cook for 1 minute. Drain the dried mushrooms, discarding the soaking liquid, chop roughly and add to the pan. Gradually stir in the stock, cooking for about 15 minutes until the grains are almost tender and all the liquid has been absorbed.

4 Stir in the reserved mushroom mixture, the cream and Parmesan and cook for a further 5 minutes, until the grains are completely tender, cover and leave to rest for 3–4 minutes. Stir in the parsley, check the seasoning and serve.

CHEF'S TIP: If your risotto is a little dry by the time you're ready to serve, stir in a splash more cream and a little warm water.

Pecorino tart
with tarragon crust

This is a really stunning tart. It has such a delicious flavour, I just serve it with a classic rocket and cherry-tomato salad for an elegant supper. It will also serve eight as a starter.

PREPARATION: 20 minutes COOKING TIME: 35 minutes

SERVES 6

300 g (11 oz) plain flour

½ teaspoon salt

150 g (5 oz) chilled butter, diced

2 tablespoons fresh tarragon, roughly chopped

½ teaspoon dried chilli flakes

450 ml (¾ pint) double cream

2 large eggs plus 2 yolks

100 g (4 oz) freshly grated pecorino

METHOD

1 Pre-heat the oven to 200°C/400°F/Gas 6. Place the flour, salt, butter, tarragon and chilli flakes in a food processor and whizz until the mixture forms fine crumbs. Pour in 3 tablespoons of very cold water and pulse again to form a firm dough. You may need a little more or less water.

2 Roll the pastry out on a floured surface and use to line a 23 cm (9 inch) loose-bottomed tart tin. Rest the pastry case for 5 minutes, if possible. Prick the base, fill with crumpled foil and bake for 10 minutes then remove the foil. Lower the oven to 180°C/350°F/Gas 4.

3 Beat together the cream and eggs until well blended. Stir in the pecorino and pour into the tart case. Bake for 25 minutes until just set.

4 Carefully remove the tart from the tin and cut into slices. Serve, while still warm, with a rocket and tomato salad.

CHEF'S TIP: Parmesan makes a good substitute for pecorino. Any left-overs are delicious served cold.

If you have time, chill the pastry case in the freezer for 5 minutes before baking blind – it sets and rests the pastry and helps prevent shrinkage during cooking.

Pecorino tart with tarragon crust

Super-speedy spaghetti bake

Pasta bakes can take an age to make – not so this one. I use quick-cook pasta and because the pasta's hot when it goes into the oven, it only takes 15 minutes to develop a crispy golden top.

PREPARATION: 10 minutes COOKING TIME: 15 minutes

SERVES 2

225 g (8 oz) dried, quick-cook spaghetti

250 g carton mascarpone

1 teaspoon Dijon mustard

175 g (6 oz) mature Cheddar, grated

6 sun-dried tomatoes, finely chopped

2 tablespoons snipped fresh chives

salt and freshly ground black pepper

METHOD

1 Pre-heat the oven to 220°C/425°F/Gas 7. Cook the spaghetti in a large pan of boiling salted water according to packet instructions. Drain well and return to the pan. Add the mascarpone and Dijon mustard, stirring until the mascarpone melts around the pasta.

2 Stir in the Cheddar, sun-dried tomatoes and chives and season. Turn into an ovenproof dish and bake for 15 minutes until bubbling and golden brown.

Super-speedy spaghetti bake

Mama's Greek
butter-bean salad

This is a lovely Greek-style salad that my favourite Greek mum, Mama Tahsia, makes. It's substantial enough to serve as a main course with warm pitta and a nice glass of chilled white wine.

PREPARATION: 15 minutes

SERVES 4

4 ripe plum tomatoes

2 tablespoons chopped fresh mint

1 small garlic clove, roughly chopped

juice of 1 small lemon

3 tablespoons olive oil

2 x 420 g cans butter beans, drained

75 g (3 oz) pitted black olives

1 small red onion, thinly sliced

200 g (7 oz) feta, roughly cubed

salt and freshly ground black pepper

warm pitta, to serve

METHOD

1   Roughly chop one of the tomatoes and place in a liquidizer or mini food processor with half the mint and the garlic and whizz until smooth. Add the lemon juice and olive oil and some salt and pepper and whizz again to make a smooth dressing.

2   Cut the remaining tomatoes into wedges and toss with the butter beans, olives, red onion, feta and dressing. Transfer to serving plates, scatter over the reserved mint and serve with warm pitta bread.

CHEF'S TIP: This dish is great served outdoors or as part of a barbecue. For crispy pitta, warm them over a barbecue then split in half. Brush the split sides with a little herb oil (mix oil with chopped herbs and seasoning) and return to the barbecue, cut side down, for 2–3 minutes – but not too close to the hot coals – until crisp and golden.

Mama's Greek butter-bean salad

Sweet-potato and coriander mash

This makes a lovely change from everyday mash and can be served in exactly the same way. I like to throw the coriander into the pan of boiling sweet potatoes for just a few seconds before I drain them. It somehow softens the flavour a little while fixing the colour at a lovely bright green.

PREPARATION: 5 minutes COOKING TIME: 20 minutes

SERVES 4

1 kg (2¼ lb) sweet potatoes

1 garlic clove, roughly chopped

15 g packet of fresh coriander, roughly chopped

3–4 tablespoons crème fraîche or soured cream

salt and freshly ground black pepper

METHOD

1 Bring a large pan of slightly salted water to the boil. Peel and cube the potatoes and add to the pan with the garlic. Return to the boil then simmer for 15–20 minutes until tender. Add the coriander and cook for 10 seconds; drain well, then return to the pan.

2 Set the pan over a gentle flame and stir with a wooden spoon for 1–2 minutes to evaporate any excess water, but be careful not to let the potatoes catch and burn on the bottom of the pan. Turn off the heat and mash well. Add the crème fraîche and some salt and pepper and mash together until smooth and creamy. Serve warm.

CHEF'S TIP: There are two types of sweet potato: the orange-fleshed and the white-fleshed variety. There's little difference in the flavour, but the orange flesh makes such a pretty mash, it's always worth trying to get it if you can. When you're choosing yours, a little scratch on the skin should reveal the colour of the flesh beneath.

Steamed spinach and pickled ginger salad

Japan is the inspiration behind this very simple, tasty salad. It's a lovely accompaniment for fried or oily dishes as it's so clean and fresh tasting.

PREPARATION: 10 minutes + chilling time

SERVES 4

350 g (12 oz) leaf spinach

1 tablespoon pickled ginger

2 tablespoons soy sauce

1 tablespoon sesame seeds

METHOD

1 Wash the spinach well, then cram into a large pan, cover with a tight-fitting lid and cook for 5 minutes, stirring occasionally until evenly wilted. Alternatively, if you've bought your spinach from the supermarket, you can often cook it in the microwave according to the packet instructions.

2 Meanwhile, roughly chop the pickled ginger. Drain the spinach well and, while warm, stir through the pickled ginger and soy sauce. Allow to cool completely, then chill for at least an hour or so.

3 Toast the sesame seeds in a frying-pan until golden brown then remove from the heat. To serve, heap the spinach into towers and scatter over the toasted sesame seeds.

Soft, bellissima
Dolcelatte polenta

Many people have been put off polenta because, when they've tried it, it was bland and rubbery. Like most grains, polenta is naturally quite plain tasting but this makes it ideal for adding flavourings such as cheese or sun-dried tomatoes, or for serving it as an accompaniment to strong-tasting dishes. In this instance I serve it straight from the pan before it's had a chance to set, but take note, it does set in just a few minutes, so make sure your guests are seated before you dish it up. I like to serve it with roast vegetables such as the roast tomatoes and rocket I pair with my Herbed Couscous Wedges (page 270) and it's absolutely delicious with my One-pot Chunky Beef Bourguignonne (page 254). Most polenta has been treated to make it quick to cook, so make sure you buy a packet with the words 'instant' or 'quick cook' on it. If you'd like to see a picture of the finished dish, turn to page 255.

PREPARATION: 10 minutes COOKING TIME: 5 minutes

SERVES 4

½ teaspoon salt

250 g (9 oz) instant polenta

200 g (7 oz) dolcelatte, diced

handful of shredded fresh basil

METHOD

1 Bring 1 litre (1¾ pints) water to the boil in a large pan with the salt. Pour the polenta into the boiling water in a steady stream, stirring continuously. Bubble for a minute or two until smooth and thick.

2 Stir the dolcelatte and shredded basil into the polenta and check the seasoning. Divide between plates and serve immediately.

CHEF'S TIP: To set polenta, omit the cheese and pour the soft polenta on to an oiled baking sheet. Spread out to a thickness of about 1–2 cm (½–¾ inch) and allow to set. Cut the polenta into triangles, fingers or squares then, to serve, shallow-fry until crisp and lightly browned or brush with a little olive oil and crispen under a medium grill – make sure the polenta is warmed through, as it is a cold centre that makes it seem rubbery. Scatter the cheese on top to serve.

Fiery chickpea
and yoghurt salad

Fiery chillies and cooling yoghurt contrast beautifully with each other in this simple salad.

PREPARATION: 5 minutes COOKING TIME: 10 minutes

SERVES 4

1 tablespoon olive oil

1 small onion, finely chopped

1 red chilli, seeded and finely chopped

1 teaspoon cumin seeds

2 x 400 g cans chickpeas, drained

200 g carton Greek-style yoghurt

2 tablespoons chopped fresh coriander

salt and freshly ground black pepper

1 lime, cut into wedges, to serve

METHOD

1 Heat the oil in a small frying-pan and cook the onion for 5 minutes until softened and golden. Stir in the chilli and cumin seeds and cook for a further 2 minutes. Transfer to a large bowl.

2 Rinse the chickpeas well and stir into the onion mixture. Add the yoghurt and coriander and stir well together until the chickpeas are evenly coated. Add salt and pepper to taste. Chill until ready to serve with the lime wedges.

Roast aubergine
and mint salad

Some people would have you believe that you have to salt aubergines before cooking them in order to remove the bitterness. I really don't think it's necessary unless, of course, they're old and leathery. Besides, most aubergines we buy today don't have those bitter juices anyway. Just carefully remove the prickly green stem, slice and use. But, beware, they drink oil like it's going out of fashion, so go easy. This recipe shows you how a little goes a long way. Enjoy!

PREPARATION: 10 minutes COOKING TIME: 30 minutes

SERVES 4

2 large aubergines

2 garlic cloves, quartered

3 tablespoons olive oil

1 shallot, finely chopped

2 tablespoons chopped fresh mint

2 tablespoons chopped fresh coriander

juice of 1 lime

salt and freshly ground black pepper

METHOD

1 Pre-heat the oven to 200°C/400°F/Gas 6. Cube the aubergines and place in a large roasting tin with the garlic and 2 tablespoons of the olive oil. Season with salt and pepper and roast for 25–30 minutes, stirring frequently until golden brown.

2 Remove from the oven and stir in the shallot, mint, coriander, lime juice and remaining olive oil. Season to taste and serve warm or at room temperature.

Roast aubergine and mint salad *with* Spice-roasted butternut squash (page 301)

Rösti dauphinoise

This is a lovely accompaniment for plain roast meats such as a leg of lamb. It is really easy to make and, as the potatoes are grated and not sliced, they cook more quickly than in the original French gratin dauphinoise. Turn to page 249 to see a picture of this dish.

PREPARATION: 20 minutes COOKING TIME: 40 minutes

SERVES 4

500 g (1 lb 2 oz) floury potatoes such as Maris Piper or King Edward

2 garlic cloves, crushed

75 g (3 oz) Gruyère

284 ml carton double cream

25 g (1 oz) butter

salt and freshly ground black pepper

METHOD

1 Pre-heat the oven to 180°C/350°F/Gas 4. Peel and coarsely grate the potatoes, ideally using the grating blade on a food processor or by hand using a sturdy box grater.

2 Lightly butter a 1.2 litre (2 pint) deep ovenproof dish such as a soufflé dish. Mix together all the ingredients, then tip into the prepared dish.

3 Dot the top with butter and bake for 40 minutes until golden and cooked through.

Peppy's rice and peas

When I was a child growing up, Sundays wouldn't have been the same in the Harriott household without rice and peas. You can use all sorts of beans and peas, but my mum, Peppy, always preferred kidney beans. Dried are best, if you've got time to soak and boil them, but for convenience sake I've used canned kidney beans in the recipe below.

PREPARATION: 10 minutes COOKING TIME: 20 minutes

SERVES 4

small knob of butter

1 small onion, finely chopped

1 garlic clove, finely chopped

250 g (9 oz) long grain rice

½ teaspoon fresh thyme leaves

125 g (4½ oz) creamed coconut, grated

450 ml (¾ pint) vegetable stock

400 g can red kidney beans

1 Scotch bonnet chilli

salt and freshly ground black pepper

METHOD

1 Heat the butter in a large pan and cook the onion and garlic for 3–4 minutes over a low to medium heat until softened. Stir in the rice and glaze the grains in the butter for 1 minute.

2 Stir in the thyme, coconut, vegetable stock and beans. Drop in the whole chilli and bring to the boil. Reduce the heat and simmer gently, with the lid on, for approximately 15–18 minutes until the grains are tender and the liquid has been absorbed. Carefully remove the whole chilli and discard. Rest for 5 minutes before serving, to allow the rice grains to separate.

Cracked tapas patatas bravas

A classic Spanish side dish, this is often found on the menu in tapas bars and always varies in each establishment. It is basically spiced potatoes and often, though not always, includes tomatoes. Patatas bravas are a delicious snack in their own right, but make a tasty accompaniment to simple dishes such as my Pecorino Tart (page 280) or Beet Leaf and Goats' Cheese Tortilla (page 278).

PREPARATION: 15 minutes COOKING TIME: 15 minutes

SERVES 4

750 g (1½ lb) baby new potatoes, unpeeled

4 garlic cloves, unpeeled

1 tablespoon olive oil

1 small onion, thinly sliced

½ teaspoon crushed chilli flakes

½ teaspoon paprika

400 g can chopped tomatoes

1 teaspoon dark brown sugar

2 tablespoons chopped fresh parsley

salt and freshly ground black pepper

METHOD

1 Place the baby potatoes in a clean tea towel and hit with a wooden mallet or rolling pin to crack them lightly. Flatten each garlic clove with the mallet or the blade of a heavy knife.

2 Heat the oil in a large sauté pan and cook the onion, potatoes and garlic for 10–12 minutes, stirring until golden. Add the chilli flakes, paprika, tomatoes, brown sugar and some salt and pepper.

3 Cover and simmer for 15 minutes until the potatoes are tender. Stir through the parsley and serve warm.

Cracked tapas patatas bravas *with* Crunchy rösti-coated lamb patties (page 264)

Ceylonese spiced runner beans

Spiced beans make a fantastic accompaniment to curry. This recipe comes courtesy of Lisa who is a real curry queen. Of course you don't have to use runner beans, any green bean will do. There is a picture of this dish on page 261.

PREPARATION: 10 minutes COOKING TIME: 5 minutes

SERVES 4

300 g (10 oz) runner beans

2 tablespoons sunflower oil

1 garlic clove, finely chopped

½ teaspoon cumin seeds

½ teaspoon mustard seeds

¼ teaspoon ground turmeric

¼ teaspoon ground coriander

2 tomatoes, roughly chopped

1 teaspoon grated root ginger

1 teaspoon caster sugar

½ teaspoon salt

juice of ½ lemon

1 tablespoon chopped fresh coriander

METHOD

1 String the beans then diagonally slice them into 4 cm (1½ inch) lengths. Cook in a pan of boiling salted water for exactly 1 minute, then drain.

2 Heat the oil in a large pan and cook the garlic for 1 minute. Add the cumin and mustard seeds and cook for 1 minute, then add the ground spices and cook for a further minute.

3 Stir in the chopped tomatoes and simmer for 1–2 minutes until softened and a little pulpy. Stir in the beans, ginger, sugar, salt and lemon and simmer together for 3–4 minutes until the beans are tender. Stir in the fresh coriander and serve.

Couscous
with broad beans and bacon

Couscous is now readily available and it's so quick to prepare. By adding broad beans and bacon you have a lovely side dish to accompany almost any main course.

PREPARATION: 15 minutes COOKING TIME: 15 minutes

SERVES 4

1 tablespoon olive oil

1 shallot, finely chopped

1 garlic clove, finely chopped

25 g (1 oz) butter

6 rashers smoked streaky bacon, roughly chopped

150 g (5 oz) broad beans, shelled

250 g (9 oz) couscous

400 ml (14 fl oz) hot vegetable stock

juice of ½ lemon

2 tablespoons chopped fresh coriander

salt and freshly ground black pepper

METHOD

1 Heat the oil in a large pan and cook the shallot, garlic and bacon for 3–4 minutes until golden. Add the butter, allow to melt, then stir in the beans and couscous and cook for 1 minute, stirring until the couscous is coated in the butter.

2 Pour in the stock, bring to the boil then remove from the heat, cover and allow to cool for 10 minutes until the grains swell and absorb all the liquid.

3 Loosen the grains with a fork and stir through the lemon juice and coriander. Check the seasoning and serve warm or chilled.

Easy pilau rice

Now, for all of you who have problems with cooking pilau rice, this recipe is really very easy and goes exceptionally well with a good curry, like my Madras Coconut, Chicken and Banana Curry on page 241. Have a go, you won't be disappointed. Turn to page 261 to see what the finished dish looks like.

PREPARATION: 20 minutes COOKING TIME: 25 minutes

SERVES 6

4 tablespoons vegetable oil

3 onions, thinly sliced

1 cinnamon stick

1 teaspoon cumin seeds

3 cardamom pods, cracked

3 star anise

500 g (1 lb 2 oz) basmati rice, rinsed

2 teaspoons salt

handful of fresh coriander leaves

METHOD

1 Heat the oil in a large pan and cook half the onions over a fairly high heat for about 10 minutes until crisp and lightly browned. Drain on kitchen paper and set aside, leaving just a coating of oil still in the pan.

2 Add the remaining onions to the pan with the cinnamon, cumin, cardamom and star anise and cook gently for 5 minutes or so until the onions are golden.

3 Add the rice, cook for 1 minute then add 1 litre (1¾ pints) of water and the salt. Bring to the boil, cover and cook over a low heat for 12 minutes until the grains are tender and the water has been absorbed.

4 Remove from the heat and leave to stand, covered, for 5 minutes, then transfer to a serving dish and scatter over the fried onions and coriander leaves; serve warm.

Spice-roasted
butternut squash

Butternut squash is a delicious nutty-tasting vegetable. Roasting brings out its natural sweetness, which is nicely balanced with the spices. This dish is great with grilled fish or meat, or wonderful on its own with a spoonful of plain yoghurt. There's a picture of this recipe on page 293 if you want to see what it will look like.

PREPARATION: 10 minutes COOKING TIME: 35 minutes

SERVES 4

1 butternut squash, about 850 g (1 lb 14 oz)

2 tablespoons olive oil

1 teaspoon cumin seeds

1 teaspoon crushed chilli flakes

1 teaspoon ground coriander

½ teaspoon sea salt

METHOD

1 Pre-heat the oven to 200°C/400°F/Gas 6. Peel the butternut squash, then halve it lengthways and scoop out and discard the seeds. Cube the flesh.

2 Put the olive oil in a roasting tin and place in the oven.

3 Place the cumin, chilli, coriander and salt in a pestle and mortar and crush together lightly. Throw the spices into the hot oil, then add the butternut squash, tossing to coat the pieces in the spiced oil.

4 Roast for 30–35 minutes, turning from time to time until tender and golden brown.

CHEF'S TIP: Try serving this with a spoonful or two of natural yoghurt and a dusting of cayenne.

Andalucian garlic bread

Have you got the Andalucian crunch bug? You will after tucking into this. Perfect for a pre-dinner nibble or casual snack.

PREPARATION: 10 minutes + resting time COOKING TIME: 5 minutes

SERVES 4

250 g (9 oz) ripe pomodorino or cherry tomatoes

12 black olives, roughly chopped

1 teaspoon capers, chopped

2–3 tablespoons olive oil

1 tablespoon roughly chopped fresh parsley

1 loaf flat bread such as ciabatta

1 large, juicy garlic clove

salt and freshly ground black pepper

METHOD

1 Place the tomatoes in a large bowl and with your thumb forcefully flatten each tomato so the flesh squashes and the seeds spill out. Mix in the olives, capers, 1 tablespoon of the olive oil, the parsley and some salt and pepper. Set aside at room temperature for at least 30 minutes.

2 Halve the bread horizontally and cut each half into 4 even-sized pieces. Pre-heat a griddle or heavy, non-stick frying-pan. Brush the cut surface of the bread with a little oil and cook in the hot pan for 3–4 minutes until golden brown and a little charred.

3 Cut the garlic clove in half and rub the cut surface over the toasted side of the hot bread. Pile on to a serving platter and casually spoon over the tomato mixture. Serve while still slightly warm.

Andalucian garlic bread

Fennel, orange and olive salad

This very simple, low-fat, Italian peasant-style salad is a lovely, refreshing accompaniment to plain meat and fish dishes. There's a picture of the finished dish on page 229.

PREPARATION: 10 minutes

SERVES 4

1 fennel bulb

1 large orange

12 black olives

1 tablespoon olive oil

1 tablespoon finely chopped red onion

salt and freshly ground black pepper

METHOD

1 Thinly slice the fennel, reserving the frondy herbs from the top. Arrange the slices on a plate.

2 Slice the bottom of the orange so it will sit firmly on the board, then with a small, sharp knife slice off the rind and pith. Slice off any remaining pith at the top of the orange, then cut into thin slices. Arrange the orange slices on the plate with the fennel.

3 Scatter over the olives, olive oil, red onion and the reserved fennel fronds. Season with salt and pepper and serve.

Simple wok noodles

This is a fantastically versatile recipe. When I serve it as a side dish, I leave it plain and simple, but it can easily be turned into a tasty supper with the addition of a little meat or some more vegetables – I sometimes throw in some left-over cooked chicken or pork or a handful of cooked, peeled prawns. Turn to page 243 to see a picture of the finished dish.

PREPARATION: 10 minutes COOKING TIME: 10 minutes

SERVES 4

250 g (9 oz) Chinese egg noodles

1 tablespoon sunflower oil

150 g (5 oz) shiitake mushrooms, thinly sliced

4 salad onions, thinly sliced

1 teaspoon dark soy sauce, plus extra to serve

200 g (7 oz) bean sprouts

sea salt

1 teaspoon sesame oil

METHOD

1 Cook the noodles in a large pan of boiling water, according to the packet instructions.

2 Heat the sunflower oil in a wok and when good and hot, stir-fry the mushrooms for 2 minutes. Add the salad onions and cook for a further 1 minute. Add the soy sauce.

3 Drain the noodles thoroughly and add to the wok with the bean sprouts, a little salt and the sesame oil. Cook for 2–3 minutes, stirring continuously, until piping hot and well mixed, but don't over cook the bean sprouts – they should still be crunchy. Serve immediately with some extra soy sauce for splashing over.

Velvet vanilla sweet-cream risotto

Okay, so it's a rice pudding, but so delicious! The round, plump risotto grain makes for a lovely texture and the flavour of real vanilla is pretty hard to beat.

PREPARATION: 10 minutes COOKING TIME: 2 hours

SERVES 4

600 ml (1 pint milk)

450 ml (¾ pint) double cream

75 g (3 oz) golden caster sugar

1 vanilla pod

100 g (4 oz) risotto rice such as Arborio or Carnaroli

small knob of butter

METHOD

1 Pre-heat the oven to 150°C/300°F/Gas 2. Place the milk, cream and sugar in a pan. Split the vanilla pod and scrape the seeds into the pan, add the pod, then bring to the boil. Remove from the heat.

2 Meanwhile, place the rice in a 1.75 litre (3 pint) pie dish. Remove and discard the pod then pour the hot cream mixture over the rice. Dot the top with butter and bake for 1½–2 hours, stirring occasionally, until thick and creamy. Serve warm or chilled. A little extra drizzling of chilled pouring cream is really nice.

Srikhand
with iced mango shards

When I made this on *Friends for Dinner*, hundreds of people wrote in asking for the recipe. So, here it is, with the addition of some Iced Mango Shards. It's the perfect dessert to serve after a spicy meal, although my family likes to eat it any time.

PREPARATION: 15 minutes, plus chilling time

SERVES 4

¼ teaspoon saffron

2 tablespoons rosewater

1 large mango

1 teaspoon cardamom pods

600 ml (1 pint) Greek-style natural yoghurt

25 g (1 oz) blanched shelled almonds, roughly chopped

50 g (2 oz) shelled pistachios, roughly chopped

40 g (½ oz) icing sugar

METHOD

1 Mix together the rosewater and saffron and set aside.

2 Slice the mango down either side of the central flat stone then scoop the two halves out of their shells. Thinly slice lengthways. Arrange on a sheet of greaseproof paper, cover with a second sheet and place in the freezer for at least 1 hour.

3 Place the cardamom pods in a pestle and mortar and lightly crush. Remove and discard the husks, then grind the seeds to a rough powder. Stir the powder into the yoghurt with three-quarters of the chopped nuts and the icing sugar. Stir in the rosewater mixture.

4 Divide between 4 glasses then chill for at least an hour. Decorate with the reserved chopped nuts and the sliced, iced mango, to serve.

Cranberry and pomegranate jellies

In my day, 'jelly and evap' was what childhood dreams were made of and I can bet that you really have forgotten just how great they taste together. This jelly is made using cranberry juice, which you can make set very easily using leaf gelatine, and will appeal to adults just as much as kids.

PREPARATION: 10 minutes + setting time

SERVES 4

4 leaves gelatine or 1 x 11.5 g sachet powdered gelatine

600 ml (1 pint) cranberry juice

50 g (2 oz) caster sugar

seeds of 1 pomegranate

170 g can evaporated milk

METHOD

1 If using leaf gelatine, place in a bowl and just cover with cold water.

2 Pour the cranberry juice into a pan and stir in the sugar. Heat the juice, but just before it comes to the boil remove from the heat. Allow to cool for 2 minutes.

3 Lift the leaf gelatine out of the water, squeezing to remove the excess liquid. Add to the hot cranberry mixture and stir to dissolve – if using powdered gelatine, dissolve in a little of the warm cranberry juice then stir into the pan. Pour into 4 glasses, then sprinkle in the pomegranate seeds and any juice. They tend to float, making a layer at the top of each glass.

4 Allow the jellies to cool, then chill for at least an hour or until ready to serve. If you like, rest the glasses at an angle in the racked fridge shelf so they set at a slant.

5 Pour the evaporated milk into a jug and allow your guests to mix it into their jelly at the table.

CHEF'S TIP: For an even more adult-friendly jelly, try stirring in a splash of vodka or orange liqueur such as Cointreau or Grand Marnier.

Cranberry and pomegranate jellies

Blue-mountain coffee rum-poached pears

I like to make these with Jamaican Blue-mountain Coffee, but your favourite filter coffee would do nicely.

PREPARATION: 10 minutes + chilling time COOKING TIME: 20 minutes

SERVES 4

300 ml (½ pint) filter or cafetière coffee

40 g (1½ oz) dark brown sugar

1 cinnamon stick

4 dessert pears, such as Rocha or Comice

4 tablespoons dark rum

METHOD

1 Place the coffee in a pan large enough to hold the pears snugly with the sugar and cinnamon and heat gently. Carefully peel the pears, leaving the stalks intact. Poach in the sweetened coffee for 20 minutes, turning occasionally.

2 Turn off the heat, stir in the rum and allow the pears to cool in the coffee mixture. Transfer to a bowl and chill until ready to serve.

3 To serve, place the pear in a pretty, shallow glass dish or bowl and spoon over the coffee syrup.

Ricotta pancakes
with mulled strawberries

Hot fluffy pancakes are something we normally associate with an American holiday. Well here's a recipe that you can make at home, looks gorgeous and tastes sublime.

PREPARATION: 20 minutes COOKING TIME: 20 minutes

SERVES 4

250 g carton ricotta

175 ml (6 fl oz) milk

4 eggs, separated

100 g (4 oz) plain flour

1 teaspoon baking powder

¼ teaspoon salt

light olive oil, for frying

FOR THE MULLED STRAWBERRIES

225 g (8 oz) small fresh strawberries

150 ml (5 fl oz) fresh orange juice

2 tablespoons caster sugar

1 star anise

1 teaspoon caraway seeds

METHOD

1 Begin with the mulled strawberries. Hull the strawberries, place them in a bowl and set aside.

2 Place the orange juice, sugar, star anise and caraway seeds in a small pan. Bring to the boil and simmer for 5 minutes, then pour over the strawberries and allow to cool. Chill for least an hour and up to 8 hours.

3 Place the ricotta, milk and egg yolks in a large bowl and beat well together to combine. Sift over the flour, baking powder and salt and stir to make a smooth batter.

4 Using an electric whisk, beat the egg whites until stiff. Carefully fold into the batter.

5 Heat a little of the oil in a large, non-stick frying-pan and drop heaped tablespoons of the mixture into the pan. Cook in batches for 1 minute on each side until puffed and golden. Repeat to make 12 pancakes. Divide between 4 plates and spoon over the mulled strawberries.

Six-minute soft-centred
chocolate puddings

These are the most fantastic dinner-party desserts. Get the puddings ready and into their tins, then chill. Take them out of the fridge as soon as your guests arrive, so that they return to room temperature, and, as you clear the table after the main course, just slip them into the oven for a truly fabulous chocolate treat.

PREPARATION: 15 minutes COOKING TIME: 6 minutes

SERVES 6

185 g (6½ oz) dark chocolate

185 g (6½ oz) butter, plus extra for greasing

3 eggs, plus 3 extra yolks

6 tablespoons caster sugar

3 teaspoons plain flour

cocoa powder, for dusting

crème fraîche, to serve

METHOD

1 Pre-heat the oven to 230°C/450°F/Gas 8. Break the chocolate into a heatproof bowl set over a pan of simmering water. Add the butter and leave to melt.

2 In a separate bowl, whisk the eggs, yolks and sugar until thickened. Whisk in the melted chocolate mixture, then sieve over the flour and quickly fold in.

3 Divide the mixture between six buttered moulds or ramekins. Bake the puddings for 6 minutes until the outside is set but the centre is still soft.

4 Turn each pudding on to a plate, then gently lift off the moulds. Place a spoonful of crème fraîche on top of each pudding and dust with cocoa. Serve immediately.

CHEF'S TIP: Why not make some hazelnut meringues with the leftover egg whites? Simply beat the whites until stiff, add 75 g (3 oz) caster sugar and beat the mixture until glossy. Add 50 g (2 oz) light-brown sugar and beat again for 1 minute, then fold in 50 g (2 oz) ground hazelnuts. Spoon onto a lightly oiled baking sheet and bake in a cool oven (110°C/225°F/Gas ½) for just over an hour until they are crisp. When cool, sandwich together with cream and chopped Maltesers.

Oaty gingered plum crumble

There's nothing more satisfying than a delicious oaty crumble with steaming hot custard. So … here it is.

PREPARATION: 15 minutes COOKING TIME: 40 minutes

SERVES 6

750 g (1½ lb) small red plums

2 pieces of stem ginger, finely chopped

50 g (2 oz) golden caster sugar

FOR THE CRUMBLE TOPPING

150 g (5 oz) plain flour

100 g (4 oz) chilled, diced butter

75 g (3 oz) golden caster sugar

25 g (1 oz) rolled oats

ice cream, custard or cream, to serve

METHOD

1 Pre-heat the oven to 200°C/400°F/Gas 6. Place the plums in a 1.2 litre (2 pint) ovenproof dish and scatter over the ginger and sugar.

2 Rub the butter into the flour until it resembles unevenly sized breadcrumbs. Stir through the sugar and oats and scatter loosely over the fruit, but don't be tempted to pack it down, we want it rough and crumbly.

3 Bake for 35–40 minutes until the plums are soft and the crumble is golden brown. Serve warm with ice cream or custard, or cold with cream.

Turkish-style apricots
with pistachio praline

My sister-in-law, Fatima, used to do a version of these delightful apricots.
I've added my own little twist and come up with a dessert that my wife says is
'to die for'.

PREPARATION: 30 minutes + 2 hours chilling time COOKING TIME: 10 minutes

SERVES 6

250 g (9 oz) ready-to-eat dried apricots

50 g (2 oz) caster sugar

4 cracked cardamom pods

1 teaspoon cracked black peppercorns

juice of ½ lemon

200 g carton crème fraîche

FOR THE PRALINE

75 g (3 oz) granulated sugar

1 teaspoon sunflower oil

50 g (2 oz) pistachio nuts

METHOD

1 Place the apricots in a large pan with 450 ml (¾ pint) water, the sugar,
cardamom, pepper and lemon juice. Bring to the boil and simmer for
10 minutes. Remove from the heat, allow to cool, then chill for at least 2 hours.

2 For the praline, place the sugar in a small pan with 1 tablespoon of
water. Heat gently, stirring until the sugar dissolves, then bring to the boil
and simmer rapidly until golden brown.

3 While the sugar is boiling, brush a baking sheet with a little oil and
scatter the pistachios over it in an even layer, keeping them all close
together. As soon as the caramel is golden, allow the bubbles to subside,
then pour it over the nuts and leave to cool and set hard. Then, place the
praline on a board and, with a heavy knife, chop into shards.

4 Divide the apricots between 6 bowls and spoon over a couple of
tablespoons of the cooking liquor. Top each serving with a spoonful of
crème fraîche and decorate with the praline shards.

CHEF'S TIP: The praline can be made up to 2 hours in advance and stored
in an air-tight container. The caramel attracts moisture, so any longer than
that and the praline will become a little sticky.

Original baked
lemon and sultana cheesecake

You can't beat an old-fashioned cheesecake, especially when it's full of juicy sultanas and has a fresh lemon zingy taste. I've substituted the heavy cream cheese that you find in traditional cheesecakes for a mixture of mascarpone and crème fraîche, so that it's nice and light.

PREPARATION: 20 minutes + cooling time   COOKING TIME: 40 minutes

SERVES 6

150 g (5 oz) digestive biscuits

50 g (2 oz) butter, melted

2 x 250 g cartons mascarpone

200 ml carton crème fraîche

2 egg yolks

100 g (4 oz) caster sugar

2 tablespoons cornflour

75 g (3 oz) golden sultanas

grated rind of 1 lemon

icing sugar, for dusting

cream, to serve

METHOD

1 Pre-heat the oven to 190°C/375°F/Gas 5. Place the biscuits in a strong plastic bag and crush with a rolling pin to form crumbs. Mix with the melted butter and press into the base of a 20 cm (8 inch) spring-form cake tin. Pop into the freezer for 5 minutes or so to set.

2 Using electric beaters, mix together the mascarpone, crème fraîche, egg yolks, caster sugar and cornflour until well blended. Stir in the sultanas and lemon rind and spoon over the crumb base, smoothing over the surface.

3 Place on a baking sheet and bake for 40 minutes until golden – it will still be fairly wobbly, but don't worry, it will set as it cools. The cake sometimes cracks, but you can avoid this by allowing it to cool slowly – turn off the oven, open the door and allow it to cool as the oven does.

4 When completely cool, place in the fridge for at least an hour or two, but preferably overnight. Carefully remove from the tin and dust with icing sugar. Slice into wedges and serve with a drizzle of cream.

Original baked lemon and sultana cheesecake

Lemon and blueberry
surprise pudding

This is one of those scrummy desserts where the top of the pudding is a delicious, moist sponge and the bottom separates out into a thick, lemony custard. Two puddings for the price of one! It's equally good eaten the next day, straight out of the fridge, although I don't expect there'll be any left.

PREPARATION: 20 minutes COOKING TIME: 45 minutes

SERVES 6

100 g (4 oz) butter, plus a little extra, for greasing

175 g (5 oz) golden caster sugar

grated rind and juice of 2 lemons

4 eggs, separated

50 g (2 oz) plain flour

125 g punnet fresh blueberries

500 ml (17 fl oz) milk

METHOD

1 Pre-heat the oven to 180°C/350°F/Gas 4. Lightly butter a 2 litre (3½ pint) ovenproof dish. With an electric whisk, beat the butter and sugar until pale and fluffy. Add the lemon juice and rind, followed by the egg yolks, one at a time until well blended – if the mixture looks a little curdled at this stage, don't worry.

2 Sift over the flour and stir in, followed by the blueberries and milk.

3 Rinse off the beaters then whisk the egg whites until they form soft peaks; don't allow them to get too stiff or they will be difficult to fold into the mixture and you will end up losing all the air you've just beaten in.

4 With a large metal spoon gradually fold the egg whites into the blueberry mixture. Pour into the dish, place on a baking sheet and bake for 40–45 minutes until risen, golden and firm to the touch.

Lemon and blueberry surprise pudding

Peppered pineapple tart tatin

A wonderful combination that works so well that when friends come round for dinner they all want a copy of the recipe. Want to know why? Just try it and see for yourself!

PREPARATION: 15 minutes COOKING TIME: 25 minutes

SERVES 6

50 g (2 oz) butter

75 g (3 oz) caster sugar

1 teaspoon cracked black peppercorns

454 g can of mini pineapple rings, halved into semi-circles

375 g ready-rolled shortcrust puff pastry

vanilla or Bailey's ice cream, to serve

METHOD

1 Pre-heat the oven to 200°C/400°F/Gas 6. Heat the butter over a medium high heat in a 24 cm (9½ inch) skillet. Add the sugar and cook for 3–4 minutes, stirring occasionally, until caramel coloured.

2 Toss in the peppercorns then, using a fork or tongs to pick them up, gently lay the pineapple rings in the pan – be very careful as the caramel is very hot. Open out the pastry and cut roughly into a 28 cm (11 inch) circle. Place the pastry on top of the pan and roughly tuck in the edges, using a fork. Bake for 25 minutes until the pastry is risen and deep golden.

3 Remove the tart from the oven, leave to rest for 5 minutes, then place a large plate on top. Invert the tart on to the plate, slice and serve with ice cream.

CHEF'S TIP: You could also try using fresh pineapple for this recipe.

Gran's baked buttered apples

It's nice to eat something sweet that reminds us of our childhood, and baked apples definitely fall into that category. This recipe is delicious, with lots of fruit and nuts, a touch of spice and a good dollop of vanilla ice cream – ooh, I might just start sucking my thumb again!

PREPARATION: 15 minutes COOKING TIME: 40 minutes

SERVES 4

4 large eating apples

50 g (2 oz) fresh white breadcrumbs

½ teaspoon ground ginger

25 g (1 oz) light muscovado sugar

25 g (1 oz) hazelnuts, chopped

25 g (1 oz) small sultanas

25 g (1 oz) butter

vanilla ice cream, to serve

METHOD

1 Preheat the oven to 180°C/350°F/Gas 4. Using an apple corer, remove the core from each apple, leaving a cavity roughly 2 cm (¾ inch) across. Butter a small ovenproof dish and sit the apples in the dish.

2 Mix together the breadcrumbs, ginger, sugar, nuts and sultanas. Carefully spoon this mixture into the centre of the apples. Dot the top with the remaining butter, then bake for 35–40 minutes until the apples are completely tender with split skins.

3 Transfer to serving plates, scraping up any pan sediment. Serve warm with a scoopful of ice cream.

Passion fruit soufflé shells

If you're looking for a dessert that's truly stunning, look no further. These passion fruit shells really do titillate those tastebuds!

PREPARATION: 15 minutes COOKING TIME: 8 minutes

SERVES 4

6 large passion fruit

100 ml (3½ fl oz) milk

1 egg, separated

40 g (3½ oz) golden caster sugar

2 teaspoons plain flour

icing sugar, for dusting

METHOD

1 Pre-heat the oven to 200°C/400°F/Gas 6. Halve the passion fruit lengthways and scoop the flesh and seeds into a small bowl.

2 Cut a small slice off the base of the passion fruit shells and sit them snugly side by side in a heatproof dish.

3 Gently warm the milk, but don't allow it to boil. Meanwhile, using a hand whisk, beat the egg yolk with about half the sugar until pale and light. Whisk in the flour and then the milk, over a low heat, beating until smooth. Cook gently for 2 minutes until thickened, then remove from the heat. Stir in 2 tablespoons of the passion fruit pulp and seeds.

4 Whisk the egg white until it forms soft peaks, then add the remaining sugar and whisk until fairly stiff. Gently fold into the custard then divide between the passion fruit shells. Bake for 8 minutes until risen and golden.

5 Meanwhile, pass the remaining passion fruit pulp and seeds through a sieve into a small bowl. Discard the seeds and reserve the juice. Pour the juice into a small pan and heat gently for 2–3 minutes, stirring until slightly thickened.

6 Place 3 soufflé shells on each of 4 serving plates and drizzle round the passion fruit juice. Dust with icing sugar and serve immediately, as they will start to sink as soon as they come out of the oven.

Basque custard and almond tart with raspberries

A Spanish sweet-custard tart that's lovely either warm or chilled.

PREPARATION: 20 minutes COOKING TIME: 30 minutes

SERVES 6

300 g (10 oz) ready-made sweet shortcrust pastry

200 g (7 oz) caster sugar

1 tablespoon cornflour

300 ml (½ pint) milk

4 egg yolks

25 g/1 oz butter, diced

½ teaspoon vanilla essence

125 g (4½ oz) fresh raspberries

50 g (2 oz) flaked almonds

icing sugar, for dusting

METHOD

1 Pre-heat the oven to 180°C/350°F/Gas 4. Use the pastry to line a shallow 23 cm (9 inch) fluted flan tin. Fill with crumpled foil and bake blind for 10 minutes until set and golden.

2 Place the sugar and cornflour in a pan and stir in the milk until well blended. Bring to the boil then remove from the heat. Allow to cool a little, then beat in the egg yolks, butter and vanilla essence.

3 Scatter the raspberries over the base, then carefully pour in the custard and scatter over the flaked almonds. Bake for 20 minutes until just set and golden. Dust with a little icing sugar and serve warm or cold – it will set more firmly when cool.

INDEX

Page numbers in **bold** indicate recipes.
Italic numbers indicate illustrations and references.

ACKNOWLEDGEMENTS

A cookery book linked to a television series can be a winning combination, especially if the programmes are made well. With a team made up of executive producer Nick Vaughan-Barratt, producer Sara Kozak, director Stuart Bateup, assistant producers Melanie Stanley and Vicky Jepson, researcher Ruth Mills, production manager Tracey Bagley, PAs Alex Johnston and Jenny Wright, editor Keith Brown, cameramen Pete Coley and Alan Duxbury, sound recordists Cormac Tohill and Andy Morton, lighting gaffer Doug Goddard and stylist Lucyina Moodie, we all knew we were doing something special and I thank them all.

An enormous and special thank you too, to my food stylist and friend, Silvana Franco from Fork for her creativity, recipe tasting and humour. Also to Sharon Hearne and Clare Lewis for their commitment and hard work tasting and preparing the dishes. It was a real team effort. Thanks girls.

I'd also like to thank BBC Books, especially my commissioning editor Nicky Copeland, project editor Rachel Copus, and designers Susannah Good and John Calvert. Also Craig Easton and Gus Filgate for their beautiful photography, Elroy Thomas for standing in, my agents Jeremy Hicks and Sarah Dalkin, and last but not least my lovely wife Clare and our very special children Jimmy and Madeleine…and our pet dog Oscar Poska.

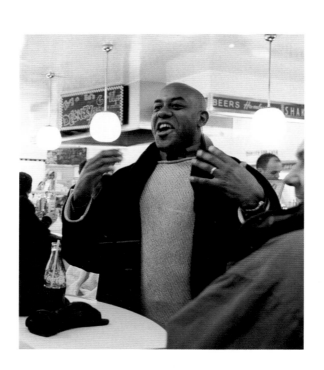